Elections

Look for these and other books in the Lucent
Overview series:

Abortion
Acid Rain
Alcoholism
Animal Rights
Artificial Organs
The Beginning of Writing
The Brain
Cancer
Censorship
Child Abuse
Cities
The Collapse of the Soviet Union
Dealing with Death
Death Penalty
Democracy
Drug Abuse
Drugs and Sports
Drug Trafficking
Eating Disorders
Elections
Endangered Species
The End of Apartheid in South Africa
Energy Alternatives
Espionage
Euthanasia
Extraterrestrial Life
Family Violence
Gangs
Garbage
Gay Rights
Genetic Engineering
The Greenhouse Effect
Gun Control
Hate Groups
Hazardous Waste
The Holocaust

Homeless Children
Illegal Immigration
Illiteracy
Immigration
Memory
Mental Illness
Money
Ocean Pollution
Oil Spills
The Olympic Games
Organ Transplants
Ozone
Pesticides
Police Brutality
Population
Prisons
Rainforests
Recycling
The Reunification of Germany
Schools
Smoking
Space Exploration
Special Effects in the Movies
Sports in America
Teen Alcoholism
Teen Pregnancy
Teen Suicide
The UFO Challenge
The United Nations
The U.S. Congress
The U.S. Presidency
Vanishing Wetlands
Vietnam
World Hunger
Zoos

Elections

by Janet Majure

LUCENT
BOOKS

LUCENT Overview Series

Library of Congress Cataloging-in-Publication Data

Majure, Janet, 1954–.
    Elections / by Janet Majure.
        p. cm. — (Lucent overview series)
    Includes bibliographical references and index.
    Summary: Discusses the history of the election process in the
United States, the modern role and influence of the media and big
money, the value of political parties, and alternatives to the present
process.
    ISBN 1-56006-174-X
    1. Elections—United States—Juvenile literature. 2. Campaign
funds—United States—Juvenile literature. 3. Political parties—
United States—Juvenile literature.   [1. Elections.] I. Title.
II. Series.
JK1978.M35   1996
324.7'0973—dc20   95-52154
                                                 CIP
                                                 AC

Copyright © 1996 by Lucent Books, Inc.
P.O. Box 289011, San Diego, CA 92198-9011
Printed in the U.S.A.

Contents

GET OUT AND VOTE
YOUR VOTE COUNTS!

JESSE
JACKSON
— 88

Introduction

WHEN AMERICANS HAVE an issue to decide, they hold an election. They vote on whether to build new sewage treatment plants, schools, and highways, and they vote to choose presidents, governors, and countless other officials. Americans vote for water district board members and rural road board members—even though the voters are not always sure what those boards do. Young children learn to vote on whether to play tag or hide-and-seek. Students elect representatives to student councils and elect class presidents. Sometimes it seems as if Americans hold elections for everything.

Americans expect elections, not surprising in a country that fought for its independence over the right to vote. Americans have been voting and holding elections for more than two hundred years. The young nation learned about elections from eighteenth-century England, where citizens could vote for representatives to the House of Commons and local councils, even though a nonelected king headed the government. The United States, though, became the first nation since ancient Greece in which the people were in charge of their own government. In creating their government, then, Americans were breaking new ground. As with any new venture, the first American electoral system was not exactly perfect, and

(Opposite page) Voters show their support for Reverend Jesse Jackson for president at a 1988 rally. In the United States, every American citizen over the age of eighteen can vote.

the country started to make changes almost immediately.

Electoral changes

The first major electoral change (the Twelfth Amendment to the Constitution) was aimed at correcting an unexpected problem with the Electoral College, a group of special electors that meets every four years for the sole purpose of electing the president and vice president. Those officeholders are not elected by direct vote of the people, but indirectly, through the Electoral College. The Constitution, as originally written, required that each elector cast two votes, that the votes be totaled, and that the candidate with the most votes become president. The candidate with the second highest number of votes would become vice president. The problem was that the Constitution had not anticipated the possibility of

Americans cast their vote in a 1988 election. Since the creation of the American government, voters have used elections to elect a candidate or course of action.

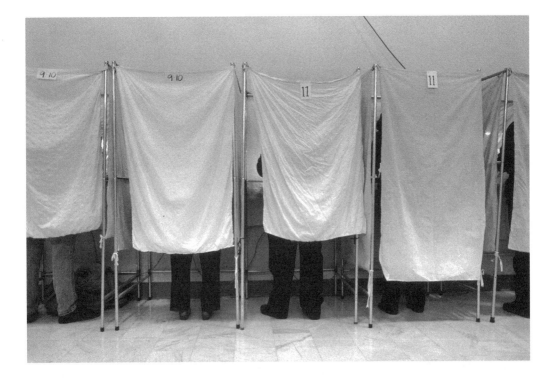

running mates—candidates who run for president and vice president as partners. In 1800 there was a tie vote for the presidency between two running mates because each elector had cast one vote for his presidential favorite and one vote for his vice presidential favorite. The Twelfth Amendment corrected that situation by providing for separate balloting for president and for vice president.

The next major changes in American election laws were aimed at increasing the franchise, or the right to vote. These changes occurred gradually through the 1800s, including a constitutional amendment in 1870. Other laws and amendments in 1920, 1964, and 1971 mean that virtually every American citizen over the age of eighteen has the right to vote in elections. During the twentieth century, other kinds of changes occurred. New technologies, particularly television, radically altered the way election campaigns were conducted and vastly increased the cost of elections.

Women march in favor of a constitutional amendment giving them the right to vote. Women did not receive federal voting rights until 1920.

Issues surrounding U.S. elections at the end of the twentieth century often involve voting practices, media coverage, campaign financing, and political parties. The question of who should bear the costs of election campaigns has troubled Americans since the early 1900s. In addition, Americans continue to address the ongoing national problems of racial segregation and prejudice and how they influence elections. The questions are complex, and the answers are not clear. Thomas Jefferson believed, though, that the American people must make their own decisions: "I know of no safe depository of the ultimate powers of the society but the people themselves;

These voters exercise their right to campaign for the candidate of their choice. Many other Americans, perhaps out of apathy, stay home on election days.

and if we think them not enlightened enough to exercise their control with a wholesome discretion, the remedy is not to take it from them, but to inform their discretion."

Public opinion polls report that people are unhappy with the Congress and the presidency, but in spite of their dissatisfaction, millions of eligible voters stay home on election day. The combination of dissatisfaction and lack of political participation troubles many observers. They wonder whether a nation truly can be "of the people, by the people and for the people" if the people, in fact, do not get out to vote.

Many people believe that the nation is at a critical point in its history. Americans who voted in 1994 showed their displeasure with the current state of affairs when they voted many officials out of office. If the current dissatisfaction with elected officials continues, election reform will remain a popular topic. Ever-changing technologies will encourage additional changes in how Americans vote. When changes are proposed, they too will be put to a vote of elected representatives or to a vote of the people. Elections are part of the American way of life.

1

History of the Electoral Process in the United States

IN MANY WAYS, the United States was founded on the principle of voting. In the 1760s and 1770s, colonists in North America objected to a growing number of laws passed by the British Parliament that taxed a wide range of supplies sent to the colonies. Great Britain was a constitutional monarchy; it was ruled by a king in consultation with the Parliament. One branch of Parliament was the House of Commons, which was made up of elected representatives. The colonies, however, had no elected representatives in the House of Commons. In 1765 nine colonies adopted a Declaration of Rights, which opposed taxation without representation. These colonies said they should not be taxed if they could not vote on whether to be taxed through their own elected representatives in Parliament.

By 1770 Parliament repealed all but one of the unpopular taxes, called duties, on supplies shipped to the colonies. The exception was tea, and in 1773 colonists showed how they felt about

(Opposite page) An election booth in 1905 reveals that only white males were allowed to vote in the early part of the century. Although black men had suffrage, restrictive laws in many states kept them from exercising the right.

13

the tea duty by throwing boxes of tea into Boston Harbor rather than paying the tax. Even at the time, colonists knew the action was important. John Adams wrote of it in his diary: "This is the most magnificent movement of all! . . . This destruction of the tea is so bold, so daring, so firm, intrepid and inflexible, and it must have so important consequences, and so lasting, that I can't but consider it as an epoch in history!"

Indeed, the famous Boston Tea Party prompted Great Britain to tighten its control over the American colonies and limit their right to self-rule. Thus began the American Revolution, which was fought from 1775 to 1781. The Declaration of Independence, signed in 1776, again and again lists the king's actions against local laws and legislatures as reasons for the states to become independent: "[The king] has dissolved Representative Houses repeatedly, for opposing with manly Firmness his Invasions on the Rights of the Peo-

Colonists protest England's rule during the Boston Tea Party. Colonists believed strongly that they should be allowed to vote for their local representatives and on laws that were to be imposed upon them.

To America's founders, here working on the Declaration of Independence, the right to vote was of paramount importance.

ple. He has refused for a long Time, after such Dissolutions, to cause others to be elected."

Simply put, the colonists wanted to vote. The U.S. Constitution, written in 1787, clearly states that members of the House of Representatives will be elected by "the people." The desire for such a right was exactly what the American Revolution was all about. The Constitution of the United States created the first modern democracy. The United States was the first independent nation since the ancient Greek city-state of Athens to give its people the sole power to determine their own national leaders and lawmakers.

What do elections decide?

Americans vote on a wide range of issues: They vote to elect officials, select candidates for office, and decide on ballot questions. Primary elections choose candidates whose names will appear on the general election ballot, and general elections choose the officeholders. Votes on ballot questions, such as whether to borrow money to build more streets, are called referendums.

The U.S. Constitution requires elections for the president and vice president of the United States, and for members of the U.S. House of Representatives and of the U.S. Senate. State constitutions specify which state and local level jobs will be filled by elections. The exact jobs vary from state to state, but most state constitutions require elections for at least the governor and representatives to the state legislature. Elections also may be conducted to change the state constitution or to modify certain laws. In some places voters can propose laws, called initiatives, for public voting. At the local level, voters elect many city, county, school, and other officials—from judges to water district boards.

When are elections held?

The U.S. Constitution says that presidents will serve four-year terms in office; senators' terms are six years, and terms for U.S. representatives are for two years. Federal general elections are held every two years (in even-numbered years, except for the first one, in 1789) on the first Tuesday after the first Monday in November. Thus, in any such election, every seat in the House of Representatives is decided. Also, one-third of the seats in the U.S. Senate are voted on in each general election, since the Constitution states that Senate terms will be staggered. That means that senators' six-year terms begin and end in different years. After each federal election one-third of senators are newly elected and have six more years to serve, one-third of senators will have terms expiring in four years, and one-third will have terms expiring in two years. Staggered terms mean that no matter what is being debated in an election year, voters cannot remove all federal lawmakers from office in one election. This system helps keep the government stable but also can slow the pace of change even when voters want quick changes. Rules for state lawmakers typically follow the pattern of Congress, with November elections every two years and some staggered terms. Timing of elections on the local level varies widely from one jurisdiction to another. Spring elections for local elected officials are common.

Who can run for office?

The Constitution requires presidential candidates to be citizens who are at least thirty-five years old, born in the United States, and U.S. residents at least fourteen years. It requires senators to be at least thirty years old, U.S. citizens for at least nine years, and residents of the states they represent. Representatives must be at least twenty-five years old, seven-year U.S. citizens, and residents of the state they represent. Rules for candidates for other offices are decided at the state or local level.

Who can vote?

The U.S. Constitution, as written in 1787, gave voting rights, also called the franchise, to "the people." However, as defined by the Constitution, the people meant only citizens eligible to vote in a state's election for its biggest lawmaking body. Under this rule, about 6 percent of adult men and no women were eligible to vote in the first presidential election in 1789. The reason for that small number was that most states limited voting to men aged twenty-one or older who owned a certain amount of property or who met other requirements. That pattern was in line with the original intent of the Constitution's writers, who as educated men and property owners thought only other men like themselves were capable of running a government.

Restrictions on who could vote, however, gradually were reduced during the 1800s. The Fifteenth Amendment to the Constitution, approved in 1870, made it illegal for states to limit voting rights on the basis of race or color, but many states used various measures to keep African Americans from voting. For example, some states imposed a poll tax to limit access to election booths. A poll tax is a flat tax charged to each voter, and many African Americans could not afford to pay it. Similarly, literacy tests stopped uneducated individuals from voting. Various laws and the Twenty-Fourth Amendment to the Constitution (ratified in 1964 to ban the poll tax as a voting requirement) sought to stop these prejudicial practices. It was not until the Voting Rights Act of 1965, however, that African Americans were assured the right to vote. That act gave the attorney general of the United States the power to send federal officials to register black voters in counties where more than 50 percent of the popu-

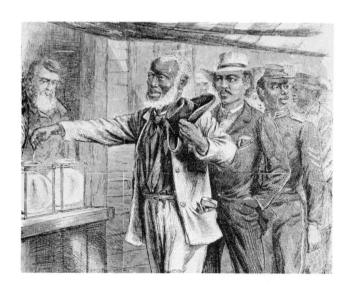

African Americans exercise their right to vote after the Fifteenth Amendment to the Constitution was approved in 1870.

lation had failed to register to vote in the 1964 elections. It also suspended literacy tests in states where less than half the people of voting age had registered to vote. That act, which has been approved repeatedly since then, prompted hundreds of thousands of African Americans to register to vote.

Women, meanwhile, had to fight until 1920 for the right to vote in federal elections. Although women had gained the right to vote in some state or local elections earlier, in 1920 the Nineteenth Amendment to the U.S. Constitution at last ruled out any laws that barred women from voting. The last major increase in voting rights occurred in 1971 when the Twenty-Sixth Amendment granted voting rights, or suffrage, to adults aged eighteen and older. The expanded right to vote is intended to make elections more fair and more representative of the views of the people. The changes in suffrage also have affected the way election campaigns are conducted.

America's first election campaigns

Election campaigns provide information to help voters learn about competing candidates. The mass mailings and television advertising of 1990s campaigns would have been beyond the imagination of participants in early elections. Indeed, for many years, it was considered bad form for presidential candidates to go out and seek votes. Instead, supporters would visit towns across the country to deliver speeches and pamphlets on behalf of their candidates. Changes in technology and the voting population have been major factors in the evolution of political campaigns.

The first real presidential campaign occurred in 1796. The United States had operated under the Articles of Confederation for the nation's first twelve years, and the articles did not provide for a nationally elected president. After the Constitution was ratified in 1788, the first two presidential elections were undisputed; George Washington was elected president without any opposition in 1789 and in 1792. In 1796 the nation experienced its first real contested race for president.

The Electoral College

As the framers imagined it, state legislatures or voters in the states would choose "electors," or officials whose sole purpose was to elect a president. The electors would meet in their states and vote for two candidates from a selection of candidates. After the electors met, they would send to Washington a list of the candidates and the number of votes each candidate received in the state meetings. These votes of the individual states would be added up, and a candidate getting votes equal to a majority of the electors would become president. The person with the second highest number of votes would become vice president. This system is known as the Electoral College. Rules provided for the House of Representatives to choose the president in cases of ties or to choose from the top five vote getters if none received a majority. Noted historian Arthur Schlesinger Jr. wrote:

> The electors, exercising their independent judgment in their respective states, would cast their votes for President, a majority to prevail; and, since no one supposed that any individual (after General Washington) would easily obtain a majority, it was expected that the House of Representatives would ordinarily make the final choice from the five highest in the list they received from the Electoral College.

That process worked just as planned in 1796, when John Adams, Washington's vice president, won a narrow electoral victory of 71 to 68 over

Thomas Jefferson. Following the Constitution as originally written, Jefferson became vice president.

From 1800 forward, however, the growing influence of political parties changed campaigns and elections. Political parties were formed to promote specific political goals and candidates, and the Constitution had not taken them into account. In fact, national leaders thought political parties were a bad idea. George Washington said the notion of party loyalty in democratic governments "is truly their worst enemy."

Parties developed anyway, and people who were powerful in their parties decided who the presidential candidates would be. Between 1800 and the late 1820s, political parties became more organized, and in the 1830s parties began holding national nominating conventions to select their presidential candidates. These conventions became famous for the "smoke-filled rooms" in which many political deals were struck.

Around the turn of the century, Republicans' strength began to concentrate in the North and East, and Democrats became more powerful in the South and West. This trend reduced competition in general elections and contributed to the

Presidential and vice presidential candidates were once elected differently from today. The original Constitution dictated that the front-runner in a presidential election became president, the runner-up vice president. Thus, in 1796, John Adams (left) became president, while runner-up Thomas Jefferson (right) became vice president.

22

Although the original Constitution did not take political parties into account, such parties formed quickly after the founding of the United States, as evidenced by this rally in front of Democratic Party headquarters in the early 1800s.

development of political primaries. In the early years of the twentieth century, several states required presidential primaries, or elections of delegates (representatives), to the national presidential nominating conventions. Those elections encouraged all the voters, not just active political party members, to participate in selecting their party's presidential candidates or delegates. Primaries, though, were largely ignored by presidential candidates and fell out of favor. By 1935 eight of the twenty-six states that had held presidential primaries in 1916 had repealed their primary laws.

Interest in primaries began to grow again in the 1940s. Several presidential candidates during that period took their campaigns to states with primaries, which increased voter interest in party nominations and primaries. In the 1950s more states began requiring presidential primaries. With a large portion of nominating delegates being decided by primaries, deal making at party conventions dwindled. Primaries are one reason that no major party convention since 1952 has required more than one round of voting to choose the party's presidential candidate. In addition to selecting candidates, delegates actively participate in creating their party's platform, which is a set of policy statements or political positions. The rise of primaries also affected the way candidates campaign for their parties' nominations.

Campaigning for office

During the early 1800s, the idea of a true popular vote was catching on, and by 1824 the vast majority of white men could vote. That meant candidates had to promote themselves to a larger number of prospective voters. However, it was considered improper for candidates to go out campaigning. Instead, candidates stayed close to their homes, sent letters to supporters, and met with visitors. In the late 1800s a few candidates traveled around the country to campaign, but with little success. One famous election in 1896 pitted William McKinley against William Jennings Bryan. While Bryan, an inspiring speaker, traveled some eighteen thousand miles in his campaign, McKinley stayed home and received visitors. He reportedly spoke to a total of eighty thousand people on one busy day in the campaign. McKinley's "front porch" campaign carried the election.

In the decades since then, candidates gradually became more active in campaigns. They began attending rallies and going from city to city to gain support. Nowadays mass communications take candidates directly to the voters. Today's candidates visit voters through television advertisements, radio ads, and personally addressed, mass-mailed letters. These campaigns are expensive. Campaign funding laws have tried to limit the amount of money that politicians spend on campaigns. The spending limit in 1992 was $55.2 million for presidential candidates who accepted public funding.

Changing election rules

Over the years, various election rules, in addition to those dealing with suffrage and primaries, have changed. In 1804 (after the tie vote of 1800) the Twelfth Amendment provided for separate votes by electors for president and vice president and modified rules for breaking ties. The Seventeenth Amendment, approved in 1913, allowed the people to vote directly for their U.S. senators. Until that amendment, senators were chosen by state legislatures. The Twenty-Second Amendment, ratified in 1951, prevents anyone from serving more than two terms as president. The

Unlike today, America's early presidential candidates did not travel out of their respective states to campaign. William McKinley, for example, won the presidential election of 1896 campaigning only from his front porch, where he chatted and met with potential voters.

Twenty-Third Amendment, ratified in 1961, allowed the District of Columbia to cast electoral votes for president. In the 1990s there has been wide discussion of campaign finance reform, and state and local governments have passed laws limiting the number of terms an elected representative can serve in office.

In less than two hundred years, U.S. presidential elections have evolved from small, exclusive meetings to massive undertakings that consume hundreds of millions of dollars and include almost every citizen who cares to vote. The Electoral College is largely ceremonial, and money accounts for as much, or almost as much, as political organization when it comes to winning elections. More changes could occur. The winner-take-all approach to elections in the United States has

Bill Clinton became president in 1992 by winning the most votes in the Electoral College, even though he carried only 43 percent of the popular vote.

been challenged by those who consider it unfair. President Bill Clinton, for instance, won a clear victory in Electoral College votes, but he carried only 43 percent of the popular vote in the 1992 election. Thus, more than half of those who voted were unhappy with the election's outcome. Also, many people do not vote at all, and policy makers debate whether government should take action to encourage more people to vote. Many changes have occurred in U.S. elections: Parties have developed and dwindled; the electorate has exploded in number and in diversity of interests; presidential primaries, mass media, and big money have changed the way candidates are chosen. Whether these changes are improvements or not depends on whom you ask for an opinion. A look at the history of U.S. elections, though, makes one thing clear: Politics and elections do change. The ongoing question then becomes, What will the next big changes be, and when will they occur?

SAVE OUR PARTY
Rebuild, Revitalize, Renew
BROWN
DARE TO CARE BROWN '92
TAKE BACK AMERICA!

2

Do Voting Practices Affect Outcome and Reflect Public Opinion?

THE ARRAY OF local, state, and federal laws regarding elections is intended, at least officially, to keep elections fair and safe from fraud. Election rules, however, can keep some voters away from the polls. Some people argue that our government's legitimacy, or its claim to being the true and legal government, is thrown into question when few people vote. Not everyone agrees with that position. They say that pushing uninterested and uninformed people to the ballot box would, if anything, result in less effective government.

When the United States was young, only a small portion of residents was even eligible to vote. Over the decades, various reforms added more and more people to the electorate. At the same time, voter turnout—the proportion of the eligible voters who actually vote in a given election—rose dramatically through the nineteenth

(Opposite page) Democrats cheer their favorite candidate at the 1992 Democratic National Convention. Despite such shows of support, some people believe that voting barriers deter people from getting to the polls.

century. The increase in voter participation, to an estimated high of 81 percent in 1860, is attributed to voters' strong ties to political parties and a sense that their votes could have a direct effect on their lives. Party ties diminished starting around the turn of the century, and so did parties' efforts to get voters to the polls. The proportion of eligible voters who actually turned out to vote stayed fairly steady through the twentieth century until 1960. Since then, voter turnout for presidential elections has fallen from about 63 percent of people of voting age in 1960 to 50 percent in 1988. The turnout jumped to 55 percent in 1992, partly because independent candidate Ross Perot caught the interest of many previously alienated voters. Few experts think the 1992 turnout indicates a new trend.

Low voter turnout

Voter turnout has been even lower in off-year or midterm elections, those general elections that fall in even-numbered years between presidential elections. The turnout in those years fell from 48 percent of people of voting age in 1966 to about 36.5 percent in 1986 and 1990. Even in 1994, a year that revealed great voter dissatisfaction, voter turnout was only 37 to 38.7 percent (depending on which estimate is used). That was the year when Republicans won majorities in both the U.S. Senate and the U.S. House of Representatives.

Some people think low turnouts cast into question the government's legitimacy. After all, Bill Clinton was elected president in 1992 with 43 percent of the popular vote, and only 55 percent of people of voting age actually voted. That means only 24 percent—less than one in four—of the adult population voted for the man who became president of the United States. The numbers somewhat overstate the small share of the population that votes, since the "adult population" that is used as the basis for turnout comparisons includes prison inmates and resident aliens (people who live in the United States but are citizens of other countries) who cannot vote. Still, many people are disturbed by the appearance that leaders of the United States, the world's oldest modern democracy, are not chosen by a majority of the people.

Barriers to voting

Although today nearly every citizen at least eighteen years old has the right to vote, people still must meet certain requirements before they can go to the polls, where elections take place. First, they must be official residents of the jurisdiction (the specific place) in which they vote. Second, in most states a person must register to vote.

The age barrier is both arbitrary (based on judgment rather than on some concrete reason) and specific. It is arbitrary because Americans have chosen eighteen as the age at which young persons are sufficiently mature to make important decisions for themselves. The age limit also is specific: A person either is eighteen or not, and nothing can be done to change his or her age.

Registration and residency rules are equally arbitrary—chosen because officials believe they must exclude some people from voting—but these rules are more varied than age barriers and present bigger obstacles to voting, especially given today's mobile lifestyles. For instance, the law in one state requires a person to have lived in his or her jurisdiction thirty days before an election, while another state requires only one day's residency to qualify to vote. The U.S. Supreme Court has stated that officials cannot require residency longer than fifty days for state and local elections, and a federal law sets a maximum

A voter's registration table at a college campus provides an opportunity for students to obtain information and register for upcoming elections.

residency requirement of thirty days for a person to vote in federal elections. These rules are intended to avoid illegal and unfair voting practices by stopping people from voting in more than one jurisdiction or from moving (or pretending to move) just to be able to vote in a particular place. Registration is another way to avoid election fraud, such as voting more than once or voting under a fictitious name. Registration means that a person must sign up to vote by giving his or her name and legal address to election officials. It is a simple process, but only about 65 percent of the adult population is registered to vote. Some places allow registration until election day, but others require registration weeks in advance. North Dakota has no registration requirement at all. The time between the registration deadline and the election enables officials to make sure that each registered voter meets the age and residency requirements.

Other deterrents

Being unable to get to the polls is another deterrent to voting. Voters who know they cannot travel to the polls on election day—such as those who are homebound or out of town—can vote by absentee ballot, but doing so requires a real commitment by those voters. First, the voter must contact his or her local election officials to request an absentee ballot, which is sent to the voter's address about a month before election day. The voter then marks that paper ballot and has it notarized, which means a person called a notary public must swear that the person signing the ballot is the person named on it. Then, the voter must return the absentee ballot to the election offices on or before election day.

Sometimes the many "districts" a person lives in can be confusing and intimidating. Local and state laws decide boundaries for voting jurisdictions. The smallest geographical voting area is called a precinct. Everyone who lives in a particular precinct usually votes on the same candidates and issues at the precinct's polling place. Neighboring precincts might have somewhat different ballots if they fall within different city council districts, for example. A voter may live in several voting jurisdictions, whose boundaries are different from one another but overlap. For example, a person might live in city council district 1, school board district 4, state representative district 23, state senate district 14, and U.S. House of Representatives district 3. Each of those districts will take in several precincts. Voters often are not sure which districts they live in, and they hear and see campaign information about candidates they cannot vote for. Voters can become confused and unable to distinguish the candidates as a result, and many would-be voters choose not to cast ballots rather than risk voting for a scoundrel by accident or taking the time to make sense of campaign information.

Language and literacy problems can discourage some voters. Whether traditional paper ballots, mechanical voting machines, or computerized balloting methods are used, a voter still needs to read the ballot. Although being literate and a speaker of English are not voting requirements, studies consistently show that the turnout is lowest among people with the least education. Most computerized balloting methods require the voter to mark a computer-readable ballot, typically by

Registered voters sign in at their neighborhood polling station before being given ballots.

filling in certain spots on the ballot with a soft lead pencil or by punching little holes in a card with a special penlike tool called a stylus. Those actions can be impossible for some people with physical disabilities and threatening for people who do not read well. In some places, voters are asked to record their votes directly on computers. That method can scare away people who are not comfortable with computers.

Errors and misuse

Many voters are distrustful of computer voting methods, which also deters voting. Some skeptics worry that computer crime could easily make its way into elections. Suppose, for instance, the company hired to write the vote-counting software could make software changes that would double-count some ballots or otherwise alter the voting outcome. Voting directly on computers concerns election watchers because electronic voting would not leave a paper trail to detect errors or fraud. In addition, the punch-card voting method has been known to cause an unusual number of invalid ballots. Up to one in ten punch-card ballots have been invalid in some elections.

"There are many, many stories of accidental errors creeping into voting processes. In many cases, it's easy to masquerade a potential misuse as an accident," Peter G. Neumann, a computer security expert, says in a *Science News* article.

Some people consider the Electoral College a deterrent to voting in presidential elections, although turnout always is greatest during those races. Each state gets the same number of electors as it has U.S. senators and representatives. Since electors cast the official votes for president, individual votes are worth more to presidential candidates in some states than in others. The most populous states, such as New York and Cali-

John Q. Adams (left) and Rutherford Hayes won presidential elections without winning the popular vote.

fornia, get more attention from candidates because they have the most electors. When a candidate wins a plurality (the most votes, although not more than 50 percent) of the popular votes in a state, he or she generally wins all the electoral votes for that state (although that has not always been the case). The Electoral College has elected presidents that did not win the popular vote on three occasions. The college elected two of them—Rutherford Hayes in 1876 and Benjamin Harrison in 1888—after those candidates narrowly won in states with many electors but lost by wide margins in other states. The third president who did not win the popular vote was John Q. Adams. The Electoral College chose him after no candidate won a majority of the vote on the first ballot.

Efforts to reduce voting barriers

The biggest barriers to voting—literacy tests, poll taxes, the ban on women voters—have fallen, but efforts continue to create truly universal suffrage and make voting a reality for every adult citizen. On January 1, 1995, the National Voter

Registration Act of 1993, which makes it easier to register in most places, went into effect. The act excludes North Dakota, which does not require voter registration, and Minnesota, Wisconsin, and Wyoming, because all these states allow election-day registration. Under the law, the other forty-six states must offer voter registration to all people who apply for or renew a driver's license as well as to people who apply for or receive some kinds of government assistance. Also, military recruiting offices are supposed to offer registration, and states must allow registration by mail. People who do not want to register in these situations must say so in writing. Although these rules apply only to federal elections, the forty-six states are expected to adopt the same rules for state elections. The new law also imposes limits on

how and when election officials can remove names from registration rolls.

Alternative voting methods

Alternative voting methods also are being tried in an effort to get more people to vote. These methods include mail-in ballots, "no excuse" absentee ballots, and early voting. Even telephone voting is being studied. With mail-in elections, voting officials mail a ballot to every registered voter. Voters fill out their ballots and mail them back. "No excuse" absentee ballots mean anyone—not just voters who cannot appear at the polls on voting day—can request an absentee ballot and cast his or her vote under the state's usual absentee voting system. Early voting, meanwhile, was used in seven states (Arizona, Colorado, Iowa, Nevada, Oklahoma, Tennessee, and Texas) in 1994. Some early-voting systems allow in-person "absentee" voting, where a person can go to an election office up to forty days before the election and cast his or her votes. Arizona, Iowa, Nevada, and Texas go so far as to set up temporary election offices at convenient locations, such as shopping centers, where people can vote early. Some Texas counties reported that up to 50 percent of voters voted early. Also, ballots in languages other than English are available in many places.

In general, these alternative voting methods are easy and convenient, but they have some major drawbacks. They are expensive, subject to abuse, and impersonal. Officials in Dallas County, Texas, reported that in-person and mail-in early voting cost $2.07 per vote in the 1992 general election, compared with a cost of eighty-four cents per vote for normal election-day ballots. Richard G. Smolka, editor of *Election Administration Reports*, worries about potential abuse. In a 1994 Associated Press news account, he said:

"Most state election laws provide for all kinds of protections at the polls. Nobody can go in the booth with the voter. . . . The ballot must be kept secret. All these kinds of things are missing in vote-by-mail."

One practice, although not illegal, illustrates the potential for abuse. Political parties in California mail absentee ballot applications to their supporters. In the state's 1994 primary election, 20 percent of the votes were cast by absentee ballot, and observers worry about voting fraud with so many absentee votes. Some people think mail-in elections and other such voting methods have an overall negative effect on government and elections because they reduce the sense of community that is part of going to the polls.

As for the Electoral College, many efforts have been made over the years to provide for direct election of the president by the people. Such a change requires a constitutional amendment. For various reasons, none of the proposals has passed, although the Senate did support a direct-election plan in 1977, but not by the two-thirds majority required to initiate a constitutional amendment.

Low voter turnout

With the many steps taken to make voting easier, one must wonder why recent voter turnout in the United States is far lower than in previous years and far lower than in most other democracies. There are many explanations, including the lack of appeal of many candidates and the predictable outcome of many elections. Also, many voters believe that their votes no longer count or that who wins or loses really does not matter. Even during the 1992 and 1994 elections, when public opinion polls reported that people were very unhappy with their government, turnout remained low. Marshall Ganz, a professor at Harvard University, suggests that the highly targeted nature of today's election campaigns may explain voter apathy. He notes that while candidates aggressively pursue some people with personalized mail and phone calls, they virtually ignore other potential voters. This situation develops because computer databases make it easy for parties or candidates to identify the people who are most likely to vote and even to discover the special interests of those individuals. Consequently, people who are considered unlikely to vote or who are firmly committed to one party do not get much attention and, according to Ganz, are less likely to vote.

Experts do know who is most likely to vote. Statistics show that the more education a person has, the more likely that person is to vote. In general, the turnout is highest among non-Hispanic, white people, voters between the ages of forty-five and sixty-five, people outside the South, peo-

ple with higher family incomes, and white-collar workers and professionals. Gerald M. Pomper and Loretta A. Sernekos of Rutgers University propose that people do not vote because they lack a sense of community—a sense of belonging and of civic responsibility—that encourages voting. To support their theory, Pomper and Sernekos point to government and survey information showing that people who have lived at one address for a long time or who attend church frequently vote at much higher rates than do people who are mobile or do not attend church. Voting rates are also higher among married people versus single people, home owners versus renters, and people whose families discuss politics frequently or who belong to groups or organizations of people to whom they feel close. Given this information, one could argue that, at least in the United States, turnout will rise if people are persuaded to increase their education levels and to take an active role in a stable community.

Volunteers attempt to increase registration among the homeless and urban residents. Registration drives target populations of Americans who typically do not vote.

3

What Is the Role of the Media?

ELECTION CAMPAIGNS TODAY, particularly presidential campaigns, no longer rely on speakers and political party activists to persuade and inform voters and to get them to the polls. Instead, various means of mass communication, often referred to as the media, are the main sources of information for American voters. The term *media* refers here to news organizations (print and broadcast) and print and electronic advertising. The development of these media has had a dramatic effect on election campaigns by allowing candidates to make what appear to be personal appeals to voters and by vastly increasing campaign costs. Those rising costs in turn have discouraged many a would-be candidate from running for office.

The power of television

Of all the modern-era technology used in campaigns—radio, television, computer databases for mass mailings—television is the most important change in twentieth-century election campaigns. Television creates a sense of false intimacy between the viewer and the candidate, since viewers can see the look in a candidate's

(Opposite page) President Clinton with members of the news media. Many commentators believe the media exercise undue influence on election results.

eye and can hear the tone of his or her voice. Ninety-eight percent of American homes have at least one television, and in 1992 and 1993 Americans watched television for an average of seven hours, seventeen minutes a day, according to Nielsen Media Research. Candidates and party officials consider the effect of television's personal power and broad reach when they decide who should run for office. Asking how a person looks and sounds on television can be as important as the candidates' political opinions. Campaign planners also consider television in deciding which messages to send; catchy phrases, emotional stories, and bright colors are easy to communicate on television.

Roderick Hart, a professor of communication and of government at the University of Texas, summarizes television's effect:

Ross Perot is taped for an appearance on the Today *show. During the 1992 presidential election Perot purchased television time during prime viewing hours to ensure that his views reached a large audience.*

Television has changed how politics is conducted and how it is received. Television has rewritten civic leaders' job descriptions, as well as influencing who runs for office in the first place. . . . Television helps form the attitudes that citizens take into the voting booth, as well as the criteria they use when exercising their franchises [voting rights]. Television explains who's up and who's down in the polls, who's in favor and who's doomed in the White House, who's faithful and who's unfaithful in the boudoir.

Facts like these are constantly being seared into the American mind by the colorful moving pictures that only television can produce.

Hart contends that television's power results in an electorate that feels informed because of the flood of information from television. That electorate, though, actually is uninvolved in the political process; the prospective voters watch but do not participate in politics.

Flawed coverage

Perhaps because of television's broad influence, its critics are quick to point out the flaws in the kind of news coverage television provides. Critics say that television campaign coverage is shallow and based too much on horse-race reporting. That is, news reports focus on who is ahead or who is behind or who is gaining ground. Such reports are based on public opinion polls and speculation by political observers, such as political scientists, veteran politicians, and campaign consultants. Candidates' views about issues, however, often are not adequately covered.

"Straightforward discussion of issues does not produce much color or excitement for TV cameras; the medium thrives on action and conflict," the League of Women Voters explains in its book *Choosing the President 1992*.

The short time available for the evening news further restricts any real analysis of issues and has led to the proliferation of carefully packaged media events staged by campaigns with well-placed "sound bites" that can be extracted from speeches and included in daily news coverage. Campaigns also strive for "visual bites" of telegenic symbols (such as large crowds or patriotic backgrounds) to convey their message.

Americans know those sound bites well. George Bush's "Read my lips; no new taxes" helped get him elected in 1988—and probably helped defeat him in 1992. Such brief and catchy phrases make snappy blurbs at the beginning of newscasts. Sound bites are intended to create an emotional response, but these verbal notes say little about how a candidate will govern.

Talk-show television

Talk-show television gives candidates an opportunity to talk directly to voters. The talk-show format appears to viewers as more impartial than ads, and candidates can talk without their words being shortened or interpreted by reporters. Talk-show campaigning exploded during the 1992 presidential race. Ross Perot and Bill Clinton in particular were interviewed by talk-show hosts and even answered call-in questions from viewers.

News coverage

While television is the most visible and widespread source of news, newspapers, magazines, and radio also contribute to information about elections. Consultants refer to news organizations as the unpaid media. These media provide coverage in news stories, talk shows, and documentaries without payment from candidates. Candidates love free media, because these media have a degree of credibility that advertising lacks. News coverage gives at least the appearance of fairness.

The public, however, has not been impressed with the news coverage they get. The Times Mirror Center for People and the Press commissioned a poll on the subject after the 1994 midterm elections in twelve states. It found that 59 percent of those surveyed gave the news media a grade of C or below for coverage during those elections. Complaints about news coverage include the opinions that the media focus too much on horse-race reporting and so-called character issues and too little on current public policy concerns and how the candidates would address them.

Character issues

Coverage of the 1992 presidential election provides one example. During that election campaign, a woman announced that she had had a love affair with Bill Clinton in previous years. Reporters asked Clinton about the matter throughout the campaign. An ABC poll, however, found at the time that 80 percent of those surveyed did not think that Clinton's private life should be a campaign issue.

In addition, many critics believe that reporting the personal lives of candidates detracts from real campaign issues. In the past, a candidate's health, marriage, and other personal problems were ignored unless they affected a candidate's or official's work. Famous examples include John F. Kennedy, whose love affairs did not become the subject of public discussion until after his election, or Franklin D. Roosevelt, whom news photographs never showed in his wheelchair. Reporters did not publicize such information because Kennedy's affairs and Roosevelt's disability appeared to have no effect on their job performance. The news media and elected officials often had friendly relations, further deterring reporting about personal problems. Jack W.

Germond and Jules Witcover, veteran reporters of presidential elections, explain traditional reporting practices:

> The standard of journalism earlier for deciding what and what not to report about a politician had been whether the alleged misconduct affected the performance of the duties to which he or she had been elected. That standard explained why it was possible for candidates for the highest public office to entertain mistresses on the side or continue to be chronic drinkers without disclosure.

Journalistic respect for candidates' privacy ended with Gary Hart's presidential campaign in 1988. Hart had denied rumors of marital infidelity and essentially dared reporters to prove he was lying. Reporters from the *Miami Herald* took him up on his dare and followed him. Only after the *Herald* ran its story and published a photo of

a young woman sitting on Hart's lap during the campaign did other news media report on Hart's romances. Editors said reporting on his activities was important because it showed that Hart was a liar, and people needed to know that when making voting decisions. Germond and Witcover say the belated news about Kennedy's affairs and Hart's behavior made the news media look bad, and news executives became "collectively sensitive about looking the other way when such activities were known about."

It was against this background of media sensitivity that Gennifer Flowers announced in the tabloid press that she had had a long-term affair with Bill Clinton. After that, major news organizations reported Flowers's accusation and additional rumors as news without the type of concrete evidence they had produced in the Hart affair. The media and Clinton opponents pointed to the alleged affairs as evidence that Clinton was of poor character and, therefore, unsuitable for the presidency. On the other hand, no one claimed that the affair, if it occurred, had harmed Clinton's ability to be president.

Similar so-called character issues have been brought up in scores of other campaigns across the nation. These issues may involve very personal matters that have no clear ties to the job, such as divorce or child care arrangements. The concern often is not that character issues are irrelevant—maybe a candidate's having been divorced five times says something pertinent about his or her reliability—but that such issues may get more attention than the candidate's stand on urgent public policy questions.

A question of fairness

The question of fairness also arises regularly. Federal law requires broadcasters to grant equal

Presidential candidate Gary Hart tempted fate in 1988 when he dared reporters to follow him to prove he was an adulterer. They did.

time to competing candidates, so that a television station that presents a program profiling one candidate is obliged to do the same for that candidate's opponent. Coverage of legitimate news events, however, is not subject to the equal-time rule. Although the law does not specify what qualifies as a legitimate news event, broadcasters generally cover public rallies and similar public events without worrying about having to provide equal time. As a result, candidates that do the best job of putting on public events often get the most coverage. Also, the minor party or independent candidates usually get less coverage because they tend to engage in fewer events attended by fewer people, and the media perceive less public interest in those candidates. Print media do not have to provide equal coverage, and editors decide how much coverage to give a candidate in their publications.

The news media are often accused of biased reporting. Sometimes a publication is accused of taking shots at Republicans but not at Democrats, or a television station seems to present one candidate in a more favorable light than another. These things probably do happen; despite their desire to report unbiased news, news gatherers' opinions are likely to creep into their work some of the time. Readers' or viewers' opinions also color their interpretations of the news they read or see; an article that one reader thinks is too pro-Republican will appear to be too pro-Democrat to another reader.

Newspapers and magazines typically do a better job of examining policy issues than do television and radio, but these print media also do their share of horse-race-style reporting. Germond and Witcover noted a difference between news media's and private individuals' questions for the candidates in 1992. "Perot, Clinton and Bush were asked by average voters on the air, and they answered, hundreds of questions, only a handful of which were of a personal nature or of the 'horse race' variety favored by political reporters and hated by most candidates," they wrote.

Manipulation of the media

News media's reliance on timely events makes the media subject to manipulation. Campaign strategists work hard to time their candidates' appearances to receive maximum exposure on the evening news. Campaigns also conduct surveys of voters to gauge voters' concerns, and campaign managers use this information to set the agenda for news coverage. They can, for example, accuse their opponent of some misdeed related to a topic of high interest. The news media often will report the accusation and then set about trying to prove or disprove it. Even if the accusation is found to be false or misleading, the candidate whose campaign made the accusation will have succeeded in turning questioning eyes on the opponent.

Advertising

Advertising, or paid media, is the other major way candidates try to capture votes through mass communication. The classic view of advertising says that a political campaign first advertises to create awareness of the candidate. Next, ads show the candidate's stand on issues. Third, ads attack the opponent, and, last, ads present the candidate as a positive force for good government. Campaigns use every means imaginable to pursue their goals. Yard signs, billboards, buttons, bumper stickers, and space ads in newspapers are particularly useful for creating awareness. Yard signs, buttons, and bumper stickers also suggest that a candidate has wide support. Campaigns use handbills and ads on television, radio, and in print to inform voters about a candidate's positions and qualifications; they send out mass mailings to inform voters and also to raise campaign funds. Campaigns rely on handbills, broadcast and print advertising, and mass mailings to attack opponents and to present the candidate as the wise leader voters deserve.

Media used to create awareness, or name recognition, often says little or nothing about the candidate's political views. Ads also may include fairly useless information, such as slogans or meaningless general statements. "The right man for the job" or "She believes in government accountability" or "The voice of the people" sound nice but do not really say much about what the candidate will do. Other information that may not be especially useful for decision making are ads that attempt to label opponents, such as ads that call the opponent a radical or a reactionary.

A supporter of the Clinton/Gore ticket in 1992 shows her opinions through the campaign buttons she wears.

Ads present the candidate—or the foe—in the way the campaign wants the person to appear, something that campaigns cannot control in the free media. Candidates can wind up looking like angels in their own ads and devils in their opponents' ads. Obviously, neither picture is true, and many people are more skeptical of advertising than news accounts. Although ads are intended to persuade citizens to vote for a particular candidate, they can provide useful information. Ads often state a candidate's position on issues and his or her qualifications for office. Ads may include such facts as the candidate's age, occupation, political party, and family status or the names of individuals or groups that endorse the candidate. The ads also may omit negative information about the candidate, such as a bankruptcy six years ago. Attack ads can provide useful information about an opponent's record (such as that bankruptcy), although such ads often leave out facts that may soften the attack.

A glut of ads

Modern technology, especially television, has contributed to an explosion in political advertising. Some people worry that the glut of ads discourages voters and prospective candidates. The concern is that voters become so overwhelmed with information, including contradictory information, that they cannot make sense of it and therefore ignore it. Some critics believe the overload of information has actually contributed to the decline in voter participation. The need to produce enough ads to counter an opponent's ads means some people who might make good elected officials do not run because they cannot raise enough money to do so. The candidate who has the most money and, therefore, the biggest advertising budget, almost always wins.

Large-scale ad campaigns can detract from honest debate between candidates, some people say. Instead of presenting their views and having to defend them, candidates may let advertising create an image through clever slogans, emotional storytelling, and attacks that have little to do with how that person would govern. "Many thoughtful persons fear that campaigns have become battles between advertising agencies rather than tests of candidates and issues," the League of Women Voters notes.

The surge in advertising has raised paid political consultants or media consultants to very high stature in today's campaigns. Consultants, rather than longtime political party participants, now largely decide how to run campaigns. A 1989 survey of consultants reported that 44 percent of their candidates were not involved in deciding which issues were most important. The survey also found that 66 percent of the candidates did not take part in deciding campaign tactics, or the means by which the campaign would try to reach its goal. One estimate says that candidates who have campaign opponents spend two-thirds of their campaign contributions on political ads and related consultants' fees.

Negative advertising

Negative advertising, in which ads vilify an opponent, often gets singled out as repelling voters. George Bush's 1988 campaign portrayed his opponent, Governor Michael Dukakis, as being soft on crime because Dukakis released a prisoner, Willie Horton, from jail, and Horton subsequently committed more crimes. Although the Dukakis campaign and others decried Bush's emphasis on Horton, Bush used the Horton issue because it had the desired effect: to make Dukakis look friendlier to criminals than to public safety.

Public opinion polls consistently find that individuals dislike such negative campaigning, but candidates continue to use negative approaches because they tend to leave a strong impression in the minds of voters.

Ideas for media reform

Campaign reform proposals often focus on advertising and campaign finance. Since 1948, when Harry Truman became the first presidential candidate to buy television time, TV advertising has become much more sophisticated and much more expensive. Fund-raising has become the first and most important campaign task for candidates. The courts found a federal law to limit campaign spending unconstitutional because it, in effect, curbed a candidate's freedom to speak. Calls for reform persist, though, because the high cost of campaigns prevents candidates with low

budgets from exercising their freedom of speech. Those candidates simply do not have the same access to the public because they cannot buy advertising time. However, efforts to require television stations to provide free advertising time to candidates have failed.

Exit polls

Some reform proposals focus on news coverage, especially on election-day exit polling. Exit polls are surveys of people as they leave polling places. Major television networks use exit polls to predict the outcome of important races, especially presidential elections. Because polls close hours earlier on the East Coast than on the West Coast or Alaska and Hawaii, announcing the predicted outcome of the presidential election before the polls have closed everywhere may encourage some people not to vote. Congress threatened to ban broadcasting exit-poll results until after polls closed everywhere. In response, the television networks agreed not to announce the results in any particular state until that state's polls had closed. In addition, the networks formed the Voter News Service, which is owned by the NBC, CBS, ABC, and CNN television networks and by the Associated Press. Since 1992 the Voter News Service has been tabulating and analyzing exit-poll results for its owners. The results are so accurate that analysts can predict the outcome of various races hours before the polls close. Still, networks have withheld the outcome of statewide races until after that state's polls have closed. Also, in 1992, the networks waited until 10:48 p.m. Eastern time to announce Bill Clinton's presidential victory, despite knowing with almost total certainty the outcome in the afternoon. These actions have drawn praise from some quarters, including the *New York Times*. Other commentators consider withholding the announcement a sham. Michael Kinsley, for *Time* magazine, wrote:

> The drama that had you glued to your TV the evening of Nov. 3 [1992] was a fraud perpetrated by a vast conspiracy. Virtually everyone you saw on-screen—reporters, analysts, candidates and their handlers—knew what everyone else was waiting to hear, yet pretended ignorance. Not just that Clinton would win, but by what margin in which states. And the Senate and governorship results too.

Media in future campaigns

The debate, thus, continues over the appropriate role and use of mass-communications media in election campaigns. These media are and always have been an integral part of American election campaigns. Their importance has grown, however, as the power and number of media outlets have grown. This growth has paralleled a decline in voter participation, and some people question whether more is necessarily better when it comes to campaign information. American people have indicated they want more information about how candidates will vote on issues. So far, neither the news media nor individual campaigns have responded in any systematic way to the voters' desire.

4

Is Money Buying Elections and Influence?

THE UNDERLYING QUESTION of campaign finance is whether money is depriving Americans of fair representation by elected officials. Modern day campaigns cost hundreds of thousands, even millions, of dollars, and the public worries that large campaign contributors may have too much influence over elected officials. The public wonders just who those big contributors are and how much they donate. The public, some politicians, and watchdog groups also worry that the high cost of campaigns may dictate who does or does not run for office.

Various laws have been proposed over the years to address these concerns. As of 1971, the Federal Election Campaign Act, or FECA, is the primary law overseeing campaign finance. The act limits how much money individuals and groups can contribute to campaigns, provides for a way to publicly finance presidential elections, and requires candidates and political groups to keep detailed records and submit them to the Federal Election Commission. The act was intended to make campaign financing more public and to

(Opposite page) Bill Clinton plays his saxophone at a campaign fund-raiser.

57

encourage candidates to seek support from more people rather than from a few large contributors. To a lesser extent, the law also was intended to make office seeking possible for people who are not independently wealthy. In short, its aim was to involve more people on a grass-roots level and to instill public confidence in the electoral system.

The high cost of campaigns

Campaign spending has been rising for years, fueled by the cost of television advertising, and direct-mail advertising and fund-raising—as well as the fees of the consultants who make those media effective. Campaign spending rose from $194.8 million for the 1977–1978 congressional election period to $724 million in the 1993–94 congressional elections, according to the Federal Election Commission. That increase of 272 percent in just sixteen years does not even include spending for presidential elections or spending by independent groups in support of (or against) candidates. In 1992 the average spending for a House seat was $543,000 and $3.7 million for a Senate seat. Such costs cause the public and experts alike to ponder just where all that money comes from, what it is buying and how it affects the election process.

Political scientists and others agree, however, that campaign spending has soared in part because more money is available. Writers Sara Fritz and Dwight Morris, in their book *Handbook of Campaign Spending*, assert that the increase in campaign spending is not the result of expensive new technologies.

"In fact, it's simply not true that high campaign costs are beyond the control of the politicians. Campaign spending is growing in response to the ever-increasing availability of campaign contributions, not the cause of rising costs."

Fritz and Morris also note that even though new technologies are expensive, technology alone does not account for the bulk of campaign expenses. The authors detail categories of spending in the 1990 congressional campaigns and find that, on average, House candidates spent only 23 percent of their money on broadcast advertising. Senate candidates spent 35 percent on radio and TV ads. The rest of the money is spent on offices, staff, travel, and other expenses. They write, "If less money were available, candidates would still be able to communicate effectively with the voters—even on television."

Who runs and who wins

Soaring campaign costs affect who runs and who wins, because nine times out of ten, the candidate with the most money wins. Seated elected officials, known as incumbents, also have an edge in fund-raising. They are well-known and already somewhat powerful because of their positions in the Congress. The FECA also allows a person to make unlimited contributions to his or her own campaign while limiting others' contributions; therefore, wealthy individuals have a clear advantage in raising money. Consequently, incumbents and wealthy individuals are the most likely to have large campaign budgets and are more likely to win.

The 1994 U.S. House and Senate races provide a dramatic example of the incumbents' funding advantage. Even though anti-incumbent sentiments were running high that year, incumbents raised, on average, $804,142 compared with challengers having raised $158,552. Taken from the perspective of the donor, only 28 percent of individual contributions went to challengers in 1994—despite voter dissatisfaction. The rest went to incumbents (44.2 percent) or to candi-

DUNAGIN'S PEOPLE

"YOU HAVE AN EXCELLENT RECORD, SENATOR!
IT WOULD TAKE AN EXTRAORDINARY OPPONENT
OR $3.5 MILLION TO UNSEAT YOU!"

dates in races for open seats, those without incumbents (27.8 percent).

Incumbents have financial advantages in addition to their superior fund-raising capacity. Political scientist Burdett Loomis observed in an
interview, "Money is important, but incumbency
is probably more important." Incumbents have
taxpayer-paid staffs who regularly issue newslet-
ters and supply other information to constituents.
Those publications, mailed with taxpayer money,
keep an incumbent's name regularly in front of
voters. In addition, candidates are allowed to
carry over money raised but not spent in a previous campaign to their next campaign. That is one
reason Representative Charles E. Schumer, a New
York Democrat, was able to enter his 1992 House

race with $2.1 million cash on hand and Senator Bob Dole, a Kansas Republican, was able to start his 1992 Senate race with $1.8 million cash on hand. Challengers can rarely match such funding, and incumbents are virtually assured of re-election. In 1988 House incumbents won in 98 percent of the cases. House incumbents in earlier years consistently won more than 90 percent of the time. Even in 1994, when "incumbent" seemed to be a dirty word, 90 percent of the incumbents who sought reelection won.

Wealthy individuals at an advantage

Wealth as a determinant of who can raise money and win elections is affected by the campaign finance law. The FECA allows individuals to contribute up to $1,000 to any candidate for each federal election, such as a primary and general or run-off election, but cannot limit candidates' contributions from their own bank accounts.

One obvious result is that very wealthy individuals are more able to raise the money neces-

Senator Bob Dole was able to use campaign money he had not spent on an earlier campaign on his 1992 bid for reelection.

sary to run a successful campaign. In the 1994 senatorial races, thirteen candidates spent more than $1 million of their personal wealth on their campaigns! Each of the top fifty contributors to their own campaigns donated more than $47,000. With numbers like those, it is easy to see why millionaires populate the Congress. The publication *Roll Call* analyzed the wealth of the Congress seated in 1995. It found that each of the fifty wealthiest members had a net worth exceeding $2 million. The wealthiest fifty (who constitute more than 10 percent of the 535 members of Congress) split fairly evenly by party, with twenty-six Republicans and twenty-four Democrats. Eighteen were senators and the other, thirty-two, were representatives. Many other lawmakers have a net worth (the value of their assets minus the value of their debts) of more than $1 million. In 1994 there already were twenty-seven millionaires in the Senate and seventy-two millionaires in the House, and dozens more took office in January 1995, according to Jamin B. Raskin, a professor of constitutional law and associate law school dean at American University.

Money and influence

Electing millionaires to office may not be a bad thing, although many Americans wonder whether such wealthy people understand the typical citizen's everyday problems. The public also is concerned that elected representatives who get large contributions from special interest groups may be more accountable to their contributors than to their constituents.

People often use the term "special interests" to describe a group or organization that is interested primarily in its own political goals without particular regard to the overall good of the nation. Corporations and labor unions, which often have much money to contribute and special political goals to pursue, have not been allowed to make contributions directly to candidates for decades. Under FECA regulations, however, people of common interests can join together in a Political Action Committee to collectively advance their company's or union's political views. Some PACs, such as the Southwestern Bell PAC, are associated with corporations, unions, or trade and similar membership groups. Other PACs are formed specifically to pursue some political goal. An example might be Handgun Control Inc., a group seeking greater restrictions on handgun ownership.

The influence of PACs

PACs can have more influence than individuals since PACs can give $5,000 per candidate per federal election, $4,000 more than an individual is allowed to give to a candidate each election. Federal candidates in the 1993-94 political season received $179 million from PACs. Also, there is no limit on a PAC's total campaign contributions and no limit on how much a PAC can spend on its own to promote a particular candidate. (Such so-called independent spending must be done without the candidate's involvement or else it is subject to the $5,000 limitation.) PACs allow individuals to amplify their political voices. A voter who strongly supports a candidate can contribute up to $1,000 to that candidate as an individual and also contribute up to $5,000 to one or more PACs that may support the voter's candidate.

Individuals, but especially PACs, frequently make campaign contributions not only to elect a particular candidate but also to gain access to the candidate when he or she is in office. The hope is that the candidate, once elected, will be available when the contributor wants to make its case on

specific legislative issues in which the contributor has a strong interest. Friends and foes of PACs agree, however, that a PAC contribution does not "buy" a lawmaker. The book *Money Talks* by Dan Clawson, et al., quotes an unidentified PAC official: "The PAC gives you access. It makes you a player....There's nobody whose vote you can count on, not with the kind of money we're talking about here. But the PAC gives you access, puts you in the game."

That access, though, disturbs many people. They are bothered that money enables some groups to gain access to officials while frustrated individuals feel powerless to influence their elected representatives. Constituents often feel especially angry when they learn that out-of-state organizations are major contributors to their representatives.

Bypassing FECA rules

People have found ways to go around FECA rules to gain extra influence through campaign contributions. One well-known way is a practice called bundling, in which someone gathers contributions from others and delivers those contributions as a bundle to a candidate. A famous case involves Charles Keating, the man convicted in the savings and loan scandals of the late 1980s and early 1990s. Keating pushed for savings and loan (S&L) regulation changes that allowed many S&Ls to make risky investments. Those investments eventually led to the failure of scores of S&Ls at a multibillion-dollar cost to taxpayers. Keating gathered campaign contributions from other people into a bundle totaling more than $1 million and delivered those donations to the re-election campaigns of five senators who could affect the future of savings and loans. Although Keating didn't directly break FECA rules, his bundling gave him much the same influence as if he personally had contributed all those dollars.

A phenomenon known as soft money also troubles campaign observers. The term refers to money raised outside FECA rules, and the sums in question are substantial. Individuals and PACs are limited in how much they can contribute to candidates. However, individuals, PACs, unions, and corporations can contribute unlimited amounts to political committees not associated with specific candidates. Common Cause, a political watchdog group, reported that the Republican National Committee, plus the national

Charles Keating bent FECA rules to give money to senatorial candidates who were in positions of power over legislation he and his supporters wanted passed.

Republican senatorial and congressional committees and the Republican Senate–House Dinner
Committee, raised a total of $45.4 million from
January 1, 1993, to December 31, 1994. The
comparable Democratic committees raised $40.0
million in the same period. Thirty-four contributors gave at least $50,000 to both Republican and
Democratic committees. Amway, along with its
executives and subsidiaries, gave $2.6 million to
national Republican committees. The Democrats'
biggest contributor was the American Federation
of State, County, and Municipal Employees,
which gave $654,070. Party leaders in the Con-
gress are well aware of who makes large contributions. Observers worry that soft money can
affect public policy—and not necessarily for the
benefit of the general public.

Presidential nominees who accept public financing of their general election campaigns have
been involved, at least indirectly, in soft-money
fund-raising. Although nominees who accept
public financing are not allowed to raise private
donations for the campaigns, some have sought
contributions to state party organizations, which
do not fall under FECA regulations. Presidential
candidates can benefit from donations to state
committees because state parties generally are allowed unlimited spending for buttons, bumper
stickers, and get-out-the-vote efforts, even for
presidential nominees. Political scientist Frank J.
Sorauf estimates that Michael Dukakis and
George Bush, who each received $46.1 million in
public financing, raised $23 million and $22 million, respectively, during their 1988 presidential
general election campaigns.

Solutions to campaign finance problems

The FECA was intended to address various
concerns about campaign financing. Indeed, it ap-

pears to have succeeded in stopping past abuses in individual campaigns, such as a $2.8 million contribution to Richard Nixon's campaign by ad executive Clement Stone and his wife Jessie Stone of Chicago in 1968. Candidates now must report all campaign contributions of more than $250, and that information is reported routinely in newspapers. Thus, voters are much more knowledgeable than in the past about which individuals or organizations give financial support to specific campaigns.

Soft-money contributions, however, are hard to track, and national parties have been required to report them only since 1991. No rules are in place to keep track of bundling. Fritz and Morris underscored why unreported bundling is a problem: "Without disclosure of bundling, voters will never know the true source of influence that is being brought to bear on lawmakers whenever they accept bundled contributions." Soft money and bundling, since they take place largely out of the public eye and involve huge amounts of money, reduce the integrity of campaign finance laws and have the potential to affect public policy. Sorauf wrote, "Soft money and bundling are the biggest threats to the integrity of the [campaign finance] regulatory system."

Public financing is used in presidential elections to keep spending in check and to reduce the influence of special interests. Rules are aimed at promoting broad-based, grass-roots fund-raising. Once the parties choose nominees, the FEC provides full funding for the major party nominees for the rest of the presidential campaign; in exchange the nominees agree not to raise money for their campaigns. Since the FECA was passed, every major-party presidential nominee has

Ross Perot talks to reporters during his 1992 presidential bid. Perot used his own money to fund his campaign and therefore did not have to disclose what he spent.

agreed to the spending limits and accepted public funding. In 1992, George Bush and Bill Clinton each received $55.2 million in public money to pay for their general-election campaigns. (Ross Perot funded his own presidential campaign that year and did not reveal his personal spending, although estimates put the amount at more than $60 million.) Money for public financing is provided by taxpayers who now have the option of directing three dollars of their tax payments to the FEC campaign fund.

Public financing of presidential elections has worked well by most accounts. The FECA has essentially eliminated special interests as major players in presidential elections. First of all, PAC contributions do not apply toward federal matching funds in the primaries, and, therefore, are of less interest to candidates. Second, after the nominating conventions, presidential candidates who accept public funding can not accept private contributions.

Proposed additional remedies

Public financing of congressional campaigns is the most widely discussed means of reducing the influence of private money in congressional elections. Polls indicate, however, that the public is not particularly enthusiastic about public financing and has shown no interest in expanding it to congressional races. Since 1980, the portion of taxpayers choosing to designate money for presidential elections has steadily declined.

Funding floors, a sort of partial public financing, have been discussed as a way to encourage less wealthy persons to run for office and reduce the influence of big contributors. Floors would guarantee candidates a base amount of public funding, and taxpayers would be the biggest contributor to a campaign.

Some people have proposed eliminating PACs, which are characterized as too powerful. Most analysts agree that banning PACs would not reduce the power of well-financed organizations but would make those organizations' election activities less public because the people associated with them probably would find other ways to finance their candidates. Sorauf writes, "Of all the dangers in banning PACs, the greatest undoubtedly is that the lines of responsibility for money contributed would once again be driven out of sight."

Reducing spending

The Federal Election Commission, meanwhile, has been considering new regulations to reduce spending for items not directly related to campaigns. Although personal use of campaign money is illegal by law, Senate rules allow members to use campaign funds to help pay for activities that are connected to their official work, and House rules allow members to use campaign money for most political expenses. Both the House and the Senate rules, however, are vague enough that a candidate could defend almost any expense as an acceptable use of campaign money. Numerous news media reports have disclosed that incumbents use campaign money for cars, meals in foreign nations, clothes, and a variety of other items of questionable linkage to legitimate campaign spending.

Authors Fritz and Morris suggest that rules should specify acceptable expenses (such as advertising, signs, phone banks, and the like during a campaign) and ban spending campaign money for permanent offices, cars, full-time staff, or personal expenses. The authors also urge rules limiting how much money candidates can carry over from one campaign to another and a ban on fund-raising in most non-election years. The underlying idea is to reduce the influence money has on elected representatives and to reduce the advantage it gives incumbents.

A few candidates have independently made personal reforms. Some have refused to accept PAC contributions as a way to show their independence from special interests, and at least one incumbent has returned excess campaign money to contributors.

Looking ahead

Campaign finance reform is difficult because the people who make the laws—incumbent lawmakers—are greatly affected by the laws. Campaign finance laws as currently written have served incumbents very well. In the absence of a tremendous public outcry for campaign finance reform, then, Congress is not especially motivated to legislate change. Still, the Federal Election Commission's hearings are a step in the direction of reform through regulation.

Some people are looking to the courts for reforms. Lawsuits have been filed in Alaska, Tennessee, and Virginia asking the courts to prohibit U.S. Senate candidates in their states from accepting money from out-of-state sources. The plaintiffs, as people who file the lawsuits are known, argue that the out-of-state contributions violate the Seventeenth Amendment of the Constitution, which specifies that senators will be chosen by the people of each state. One reason for passage of the Seventeenth Amendment was to counter the influence of special interest spending on state legislators, who chose U.S. senators under the original Constitution. Raskin says the lawsuits could give the Supreme Court a chance to overturn its 1976 decision that banned limits on campaign spending and limits on contributions to one's own campaign.

PRO-CHOICE
PRO-CLINTON
CHOICE
CLINTON
ELECT
AROL
MOSELEY
RAUN
U.S. SENATE
PRO-CHOICE
PRO-CLINTON
PRO-CH
PRO-CLI
BILL CLINTON

5

Are Political Parties the Problem or the Solution?

PARTY POLITICS, ALSO known as partisan politics, have always been denounced by American politicians and voters. Eighteenth-century American politicians and philosophers warned against the dangers of political parties, thought of in the nation's earliest days as antidemocratic factions favoring mob rule. George Washington, in his farewell address to Congress in 1796, said, "Let me now . . . warn you in the most solemn manner against the baneful effects of the spirit of party." Almost two hundred years later, in 1994, public officials denounced partisan politics as the cause of government inaction. Vin Weber, a former Republican congressman from Minnesota, said in an Associated Press report, "People see the political parties as a barrier to participating in society rather than a conduit."

(Opposite page) Pro-choice supporters show their approval of Clinton in 1992. Some commentators argue that special interest groups have more influence in elections than political parties.

The roles of political parties

Parties, however, may well have been unavoidable, because they perform functions essential to

73

the electoral process. They give voters some sense of candidates' loyalties and political positions. Parties work to motivate voters and to inform them about the strengths of their candidates and the weaknesses of their foes. On a broader scale, parties help keep government stable, because party ties provide structure and loyalties within and between bodies of elected representatives. On the other hand, parties also provide a mechanism to promote change. When individuals or groups become unhappy with the current state of affairs, they can become involved in party politics. People often can work for change more effectively as a group than as individuals working alone. For example, both the National Right to Life Committee and its various state affiliates and the Christian Coalition worked effectively within the Republican Party to move the party in a more conservative direction during the 1980s and 1990s and to help put conservative politicians in leadership positions in Congress and in state legislatures. Parties also help finance candidates' election campaigns.

Filling jobs

Parties do not touch personal lives as they once did. In the late 1800s and early 1900s, parties were important to voters because they provided jobs. During that time, thousands of governmental jobs were filled on a patronage basis. That meant the party in power had the privilege of filling those jobs with party loyalists, friends, and relatives. Also, if a person had a problem with a public service such as trash pickup, he or she would frequently complain to a party boss rather than an elected official. Most public service jobs these days fall under civil service rules, meaning the jobs are filled based on merit and are not subject to political whim. Still, parties in power always have at least a few jobs to hand out.

Parties also have been viewed as the only unifying force in the American political system, which was designed to divide power. Historian Walter Dean Burnham in *The American Party Systems* says that "party is a vitally important vehicle for simplifying and unifying public choice." Under the U.S. Constitution, the executive branch (the presidency), the legislative branch (the Congress), and the judicial branch (the courts) each has a share of national power. In the absence of parties, these governmental branches could well be the power bases for individuals whose primary goal was building up their own power. The government could be in disarray if the president, the Speaker of the House, and the chief justice of the

A Republican convention in 1912. Early in the century, the party that won an election was able to employ thousands of supporters with government jobs.

Supreme Court fought among themselves to be
the most powerful person in government. Instead,
party loyalties tie the president to lawmakers in
Congress, and judges owe their jobs in part to
party involvement.

The decline of party identification

Although political parties are an integral part
of American elections, parties have lost a great
deal of their influence in the last half of the twentieth century. This loss has occurred partly because of technology. The rise of television and
computers has lessened the extent to which individual candidates rely on their parties to get
elected. At one time, party officials handpicked
candidates. Nowadays, a person's ability to get
elected is more a product of how much money he
or she can raise. That money allows a candidate
to bypass the party and go directly to voters with
the campaign message. That point was made
clear in California in 1994. Republican Michael
Huffington nearly beat incumbent Democratic
senator Dianne Feinstein in her bid for reelection
because he spent millions of dollars of his own
money on his campaign, even as high-ranking
Republicans endorsed Feinstein. With less power
to choose and elect candidates and with less
power to hand out jobs, parties simply have less
power in the electoral process than they did fifty
or one hundred years ago.

Political parties, meanwhile, have lost influence with voters. Few individuals look to parties
for jobs or for help. Also, the public sees little
difference between the two major political parties, the Democratic and Republican Parties.
Party affiliation, therefore, may have little value
to a voter trying to decide whom to vote for, and
individuals have fewer reasons to belong to a political party, or perhaps even to identify with one.

In fact, political scientist Martin P. Wattenberg says, "The decline of public affection for the parties has not been due to any greater negative feelings about the Democrats and Republicans but rather to an increasing sense that the parties no longer matter much in the governmental process."

More people than ever are calling themselves independents. A 1990 Gallup poll found that 39 percent of respondents said they were Democrats, 31 percent called themselves Republican, and 30 percent said they were independents. By contrast, a study said that in 1952 only about 23 percent called themselves independents, while about 47 percent said they were Democrats and about 28 percent said they were Republicans. The rest, about 3 percent, considered themselves apolitical, or not interested in politics. (The numbers add up to 101 because of rounding.) In most states, though, a person has to declare himself or herself a Democrat or Republican to vote in primary elections. In locales where one party dominates, the winner of that party's primary has little general election opposition, and primaries are very

Democrat Dianne Feinstein barely won her bid for reelection to the Senate, even though she was endorsed by many in the Republican Party. Her challenger, Michael Huffington, almost won the election without his party's support by using his personal fortune to finance his campaign.

important in those places. Elsewhere, though, independents are content to sit out primaries and cast their votes in the general election. Meanwhile, the number of single-issue political groups, such as those promoting environmental causes or civil rights for homosexuals, has grown. These groups endorse candidates who support the group's particular interest, regardless of the candidate's party, and then the groups work to help elect their candidates.

Political uncertainty

Some political scientists think American politics has become more unpredictable as a result of parties' declining influence. If voters had clear party loyalties, the president and Congress would be expected to be from the same party and public policy would be expected to follow party policy.

Some observers believe Bill Clinton's presidential victory was less a vote of confidence in his abilities than a vote against then-president George Bush.

Instead, voters in recent years have repeatedly elected presidents and congresses of opposing parties. The result is often political uncertainty because the president and party leaders in Congress often act as foes, more interested in "beating" their opponents than in working together for good public policy. Democrats dominated Congress during the Reagan, Bush, Nixon, and Ford Republican presidencies (except for two years in which the Republicans were the majority party in the Senate). Since Democrat Bill Clinton became president, the Congress has become Republican dominated. The one-term presidencies of Jimmy Carter and George Bush are cited as evidence of political instability, since incumbent presidents historically have been very strong candidates.

The nation's switch to a Democratic president and a Republican Congress in the 1994 elections is not a sign that Americans have become more party conscious or more favorable toward Republicans, observers say. Rather, the 1994 election showed that people were generally dissatisfied with the way the government is being run. The November 21, 1994, issue of *U.S. News & World Report* said after the election: "Exit polls conducted by Voter News Service found that many voters cast ballots *against* the president and his party, not *for* the Republicans, and are not eager for a sharp swing to the right or a wholesale dismantlement of the federal government." In other words, voters indicated that they do not think that either major party is the answer to government ills.

Are there differences between the parties?

With parties playing less important roles and with the public being dissatisfied with government under the existing parties, people often ask, Why does not someone start a third party? The answer to that question lies in the Constitution,

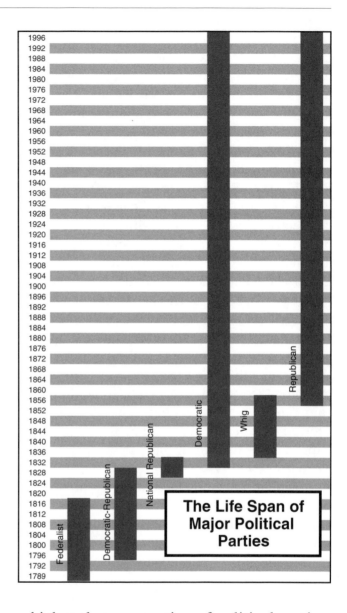

The Life Span of Major Political Parties

which makes no mention of political parties. Elections in the United States are winner-take-all events. In other words, whoever gets the most votes wins. If candidates from parties compete for an office, the candidate with the most votes wins, even if he or she gets less than a majority (a plurality) of all votes cast. For example, if Party A gets 40 percent of the votes, Party B gets 30 percent, and Party C gets 30 percent, that means candidates from parties B and C combined won 60 percent—more than a majority. Nevertheless, Party A wins the election. This kind of result encourages parties B and C to get together to beat A in the next election. Thus, there always is a tendency to form a party that can gather more than half, or a majority, of the votes.

Two parties dominate

Since parties first appeared in the United States, the country for all practical purposes has always had two dominant parties with a handful of minor parties in the background. However, the dominant parties have not been strongly ideological, that is, promoting one point of view, because they have needed broad appeal in order to win a majority of votes. The modern day Democratic Party traditionally has been identified with working people, organized labor, and various ethnic groups, particularly African Americans and Jews. The Republican Party traditionally has been identified with business, financial, and rural interests. In the 1990s Republicans called the Democrats "tax-and-spend liberals," referring to the Democratic support of government social programs, such as Head Start. Democrats label Republicans "borrow-and-spend conservatives," referring to the tendency of recent Republican administrations (especially Ronald Reagan's) to increase government borrowing while increasing spending on defense and tax breaks for businesses. In fact, though, both parties have conservative and liberal members. Both parties have platforms, or general policy positions, that take a broad approach, generally not tying themselves too tightly to any particular viewpoint and allowing themselves to woo large portions of the population. Neither party, though, has a clearly identifiable political ideology.

Other parties also have long been a part of the American political scene, but none has had enduring influence in the face of the two dominant parties. These so-called third parties have brought ideas into the public arena that later have become public policy. Their ideas have included the graduated income tax, popular election of senators (they originally were elected by state legislatures), women's suffrage, and the minimum wage. The third parties, unlike the dominant parties, have not cast their nets as wide in fishing for supporters, and thus have not been able to endure in the winner-take-all world of American politics. No third-party candidate has ever won the presidency. Ross Perot's bid in 1992 (when he won 18.9 percent of the popular vote) was the best showing of any third-party candidate since Theodore Roosevelt received 27.4 percent of the

Ross Perot made himself a national figure when he won 18.9 percent of the popular vote in 1992.

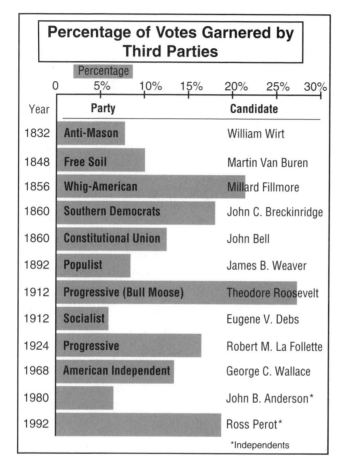

Percentage of Votes Garnered by Third Parties

Year	Party	Candidate
1832	Anti-Mason	William Wirt
1848	Free Soil	Martin Van Buren
1856	Whig-American	Millard Fillmore
1860	Southern Democrats	John C. Breckinridge
1860	Constitutional Union	John Bell
1892	Populist	James B. Weaver
1912	Progressive (Bull Moose)	Theodore Roosevelt
1912	Socialist	Eugene V. Debs
1924	Progressive	Robert M. La Follette
1968	American Independent	George C. Wallace
1980		John B. Anderson*
1992		Ross Perot*

*Independents

popular vote in 1912 as the Progressive, or Bull Moose, candidate.

The stability of the dominant parties in the 1990s has been a source of frustration for voters unhappy with the federal government. Voters see both parties as unable to solve the nation's problems, but efforts to form broad-based third parties have failed. One reason is that the Democratic and Republican Parties are institutionalized; they are specifically provided for in most state and federal election laws. Members of other parties have to do more than the Democrats or Republicans even to get their names on election ballots.

Since recruiting and electing candidates to office is a political party's most important function, the public presence of parties is much greater during election years. At the local level, many elections are nonpartisan, or conducted without official party participation. The Democratic and Republican Parties are institutions in state and federal elections, though. State laws usually define exactly how parties can conduct their election business. State laws dictate, for example, whether candidates are chosen by party caucuses or by primary elections. They also dictate who is eligible to participate in the caucuses or primaries. In some states, voters must register in advance as a Republican or Democrat to vote in primaries. In other states, voters can declare their party identification at the polls. In states with caucuses, party members meet in their precincts to select their party's candidate in the general election.

Choosing and supporting candidates

Although a person does not need to have party backing to run for office, parties often encourage and support their candidates. Third-party or independent candidates generally lack statewide organizations to help them get elected to a state office or to Congress. Also, most states have requirements that third-party or independent candidates must meet. A typical requirement is for such candidates to acquire the signatures of thousands of registered voters on nominating petitions. These rules make it harder for such candidates to get on the ballot. The rules, however, make it easier for voters, because they do not have to face a ballot with a dozen candidates, most of whom are unfamiliar.

Parties' role in choosing candidates probably is most visible, though, during presidential campaigns. Democrat and Republican presidential hopefuls pass through a series of state caucuses and primaries hoping to get their parties' nomination for the presidency. Parties no longer nominate candidates through insider deal making at national conventions, as was long the case. In recent years, the state primaries and caucuses have decided the parties' nominees. National party conventions in essence "crown" the winning nominee and play an important and highly visible role in presidential campaigns. Conventions allow party members to rally behind their nominee in a show of public unity and to decide on the party platform.

The role of political parties in government

One might wonder why the American public continues to look upon the existing parties with suspicion. A 1994 poll by the Times Mirror Center for the People & the Press found that 53 percent of Americans think establishing a third party is a good idea, up from 43 percent a decade earlier. John King, writing for the Associated Press, said:

> The reasons for this discontent are many, from anxiety over global economic turmoil and stagnant wages to the increasingly held view that there is little difference between the two national parties— that both are captive of wealthy special interests and deaf to the concerns of average Americans.

Those attitudes actually may reflect the decline of party power rather than indicate parties are too powerful. Indeed, Wattenberg says the most frequently cited consequences of the decline of parties are the rise of special interest groups and the decline in the notion that Congress or either party as a group is responsible for good government.

Public opinion polls indicate a dissatisfaction with the way parties operate in government, rather than in elections. Americans for years have been watching popular legislation fall hostage to party politics in Congress. Republicans routinely oppose legislation proposed by Democrats, and Democrats oppose laws proposed by Republicans. Rules in the U.S. Senate effectively allow any member to halt action on any proposed law, or bill, unless the membership overwhelmingly counteracts the move. Members in the House of Representatives are also able to use various procedural rules to bog down or confuse the legislative process. Two weeks into the new Republican-dominated Congress in 1995, Katharine Q. Seelye of the *New York Times* described what happens when lawmakers use such rules to muddle the process: "Using the same disruptive tactics perfected by [Republican] Newt Gingrich during his rise to power, Democrats brought the House chamber to the brink of chaos Wednesday." This kind of behavior does not give citizens confidence that party politics foster effective government. A 1994 issue of *U.S. News & World Report* says that four of five voters disapprove of the way Congress operates and that "voters also resent Capitol Hill's partisan gamesmanship."

Should parties be reformed?

Questions persist as to whether political parties serve the public benefit. Some commentators would argue that stronger parties would encourage better government. That school of thought suggests that stronger parties would mean electing candidates based on party positions rather than on the strength of the candidate's personality or special-interest backing. In that case, voters should have a better idea of how their elected officials will behave in office, and parties would have more power to enforce the platform on which the officials were elected. Others would argue that party politics are responsible for "Washington gridlock," in which nothing gets done because the parties will not cooperate with each other.

Changes in the way Congress operates, rather than changes in parties themselves, would have a greater effect on reducing government inaction.

Congress could, for example, change the rules so that important committee chairpersons are assigned on the basis of overall seniority. As it is, members of the majority party serve as committee chairs. Congress could also change the rules that allow individual members to delay or stop votes on controversial bills. Congress also could stop allowing amendments to be added to bills.

National party structures, however, are not sufficiently powerful anymore to force representatives and senators to take such steps. Few think that parties can be made more powerful in the age of television and other media that allow candidates to get elected without party backing. Many observers feel, however, that elections and politics in the United States are at a critical point and that something must change because the government needs the support of the people to maintain its authority.

Some people think that the decline of political parties has cost Americans an important link with their elected officials. Indeed, one political scientist says the ordinary American is not adequately represented when elections are candidate dominated, that is, when elections are between well-financed candidates with little loyalty to parties and their platforms. Walter Dean Burnham wrote in the foreword to *The Decline of American Political Parties:*

> [P]ure candidate-domination of elections is a recipe for irresponsible, unaccountable performance in office, and is equally a recipe for domination of the political order by the haves at the expense of the have-nots. This candidate-domination, while preserving the forms of democracy, negates its substance.

The question now is whether individual citizens or political parties will act to change that state of affairs.

6

Should Alternatives to Winner-Take-All Elections Be Tried?

U.S. ELECTIONS REALLY are quite simple. A voter gets a ballot and indicates his or her favorite candidate for each office. Election officials collect all the ballots, add up the votes for each candidate, and declare the person with the most votes the winner. The pattern holds true for nearly every federal, state, local, primary, or general election.

While simplicity is elegant, it is not always fair, at least where elections are concerned. Despite the Voting Rights Acts of the 1960s, minority groups often have been unable to elect one of their members to office. Also, in races with more than two major candidates, it is possible for the leading candidate to win with considerably less than a majority of the vote. In such cases, as in the 1992 presidential campaign, some people will complain that more than half of the voters are not being represented. Another concern is the low voter turnout

89

Some observers believe that low voter turnout, while frustrating, is not a cause for dismay. It may prove that Americans ultimately have confidence in the system.

that has been the pattern in the United States for the past thirty years. If low turnout is a result of people's feelings that their views are not being represented, then some people suggest that the electoral system needs to be changed. Governments need citizen support to be viewed as legitimate. The American system is not the only way to elect leaders, and in fact, other countries use various methods to elect their leaders.

The proportional representation alternative

The American system is known as winner-take-all or first-past-the-post, terms that reflect the system's parallels to a horse race: Whoever is ahead at the end of the race wins, and the winner does not share the prize with anyone. The system is so ingrained in the United States that suggestions to consider other methods have been decried as antidemocratic or contrary to the principle of one man, one vote. In fact, the winner-take-all system is in the minority among world democracies, but the countries best known for using it are major players in world economics and politics. Those countries are the United States, Canada, and Great Britain.

The norm in Europe and Latin America, however, is some form of proportional representation. Under proportional representation, electoral districts have more than one elected representative. Winners are selected in proportion to the number of votes cast for the candidates or their parties. For example, a city might elect its ten city council members at large, meaning every voter in the city votes on the same list of candidates (instead of the city being divided up into ten smaller districts, each with its own list of candidates). If Party A's candidates together gain 40 percent of the vote, then four (or 40 percent) of the city council seats will be filled by Party A members. If Party B gets 30 percent of the vote, it gets three (or 30 percent) of the seats. If Party C gets 20 percent, it gets two seats, and an independent candidate who wins 10 percent of the vote would hold one seat. More than two parties are typical in places with proportional representation.

Variations

Many variations exist for holding proportional representation elections, and for tabulating the votes. In some systems, citizens vote for party lists. In others, voters indicate their preferences, ranking the candidates 1, 2, 3, and so on. Other systems decide the winners in multirepresentative districts by applying various formulas to the number of votes cast. Some countries use a combination of election methods. Spain uses winner-take-all for one house of its parliament and a proportional representation method for its other house. Germany also uses a combination of methods. No matter which method of proportional representation is used, however, most observers agree that proportional representation at least appears to represent minority political interests more fairly. That is because if a minority

In Latin America, voters rely on a system called proportional representation. In this type of system, candidates are chosen by what percentage vote they or their party pulled.

party wins 30 percent of the votes in an election, that party gets 30 percent of the seats in the law-making body. In the United States, a party with 30 percent of the votes probably would not have any representatives, even though 30 percent is a significant minority. Americans interested in the idea of proportional representation have formed an organization in Washington, D.C., called the Center for Voting and Democracy. The organization's literature states:

> Implementing proportional voting systems at all levels of government would increase vitality in our democracy, ensure fairer representation of our society's diversity in elected bodies and assist local, state and national governments in their efforts toward solving the complex and contentious issues facing our nation. PR [proportional representation] systems are not a panacea, but they could provide dramatic improvements in how Americans interact with their government.

Proportional representation has its drawbacks and its opponents. Critics most often point to unstable and factional governments, with Italy and Poland as prime examples. In 1993 Poland had twenty-nine parties represented in its main legislative body, making any agreement on policy issues difficult. The multiparty legislative body in Italy chooses that nation's government. As a result (and since this form of government does not have a nationally elected president or fixed terms of office, as in the United States), Italy had fifty-two different national governments—more than one a year—in power between 1945 and 1993. In 1993 Italians approved electoral changes so that most members of its parliament are now elected in winner-take-all elections.

Some forms of proportional representation tend to give big parties more than their share of power; others give disproportionate power to small parties. Another problem under some forms of proportional representation is the undue power it gives to political party bosses. Experience has shown that proportional representation is no guarantee of good government—or of bad government. The *Economist*, a British periodical, reported:

> The choice looks clear: good government [in places with winner-take-all elections] or fair representation [with proportional representation]? In fact, not so. British governments have often been feeble; Israel's [proportional representation governments] often decisive, even fierce. Italy's governments are unstable and inept; not so Germany's, although the Bundestag they rest on is shaped by PR [proportional representation].

Cumulative voting

Members of Congress have shown no interest in proportional representation, but examples of a similar system called cumulative voting do exist in the United States. Cumulative voting, like proportional representation, requires a jurisdiction to have several elected representatives. An example might be a city with five at-large school board members (instead of one member being elected from each of five geographic districts). Citizens vote differently, though, in cumulative voting. Under this system, each voter can cast as many votes as there are representatives to be elected. The voter can distribute his or her votes in any way among the candidates. Thus, in the example above, a person would cast five votes if all five school board seats were vacant. The person could cast all five votes for one candidate if the person felt very strongly about that particular candidate. Voters could also vote for five different candidates or spread their five votes among three or four candidates.

Cumulative voting has been promoted as a way to provide minority political representation. It would allow people in a political minority, such as Libertarian Party members, to band together in casting all their votes for a Libertarian Party candidate. If the party was supported by 15 percent

Voters wait at the polls to cast their vote. Different forms of representative voting are being explored to encourage minorities and minority parties to have more say in government.

of the population, for instance, it probably would never be able to win a seat in a winner-take-all election. With cumulative voting, however, the resulting legislative body might wind up with a Libertarian member. Cumulative voting, similarly, has been suggested as an alternative to awkwardly drawn geographic districts designed to assure representation to racial minorities. Jurisdictions that historically have kept minority groups out of elective office now are required to create districts where minorities are in the majority. These districts sometimes are called majority-minority districts. As a result, at-large jurisdictions have been divided into districts. The districts' boundaries are drawn to assure that African Americans or some other minority group holds the majority in some district or districts. Also, congressional districts in some states have been redrawn to create majority-minority districts. These sometimes oddly shaped districts have been criticized as unfair to the majority population. Such districts also have been criticized because they encourage racial separation.

Richard H. Pildes, a law professor at the University of Michigan, wrote in 1993 that cumulative voting does away with the need for specially drawn districts. "Voters voluntarily define their own interests and the voting affiliations that best promotes them," he wrote. Majority-minority districts, on the other hand, assume that all black people or Hispanic people have the same political interests. With cumulative voting, he said, "Any group that feels the need to vote cohesively is able to do so."

Examples of cumulative voting

Chilton County, Alabama, has used cumulative voting since 1988 as a means to address the absence of African Americans on the county's formerly five-seat county commission. African

Americans make up about 12 percent of the county population and are widely dispersed through the county, which makes redistricting impractical. When cumulative voting was instituted, the commission was increased to seven members, and one black Democrat was elected. Republicans, who are outnumbered about 3 to 1 in primary elections, also benefited from cumulative voting, winning three seats on the commission in 1988. They won only two in 1992. By 1995 Alamagordo, New Mexico, had used cumulative voting for three election years. The system brought into office the city's first Hispanic council member in decades, despite the city's having about 24 percent Hispanic residents. Since 1991, Peoria, Illinois, has also used cumulative voting as a means to improve minority representation on its at-large council, although with a slightly different method. None of these places has used the method enough to answer all questions about its problems and benefits.

Other ideas for gaining citizen participation

Changing the U.S. election system to proportional representation or cumulative voting would be a drastic switch. Other ideas exist, though, that are perhaps less dramatic and that also have as their goal increased citizen participation and confidence in elections. These ideas include a none-of-the-above option on ballots, electronic town halls, and various forms of direct democracy.

Since 1976 ballots in Nevada elections have included a none-of-the-above option on ballots. This option allows voters who are dissatisfied with the selection of candidates to choose None of the Above instead of a candidate. The Nevada scheme is nonbinding. That means votes for None of the Above do not affect the outcome of an election, except for taking votes away from the

A sign reveals the public's frustration with incumbents, suggesting that any candidate would be better than the ones currently in office.

candidates. Still, proponents of the option say a strong none-of-the-above vote forces candidates to determine why voters are so dissatisfied. Some people think the idea should be carried further. They think that when None of the Above wins a plurality or majority of votes, a new election should be called. Candidates who lost to None of the Above would be barred from running in the follow-up election. A similar method has been used in the former Soviet Union, where voters can cross off the names of candidates they reject. According to one report, new elections with new candidates had to be held in two hundred (out of fifteen hundred) contests for the Congress of People's Deputies in 1989. Proponents say the none-of-the-above option would reduce the advantage of incumbents seeking reelection. John H. Fund, a *Wall Street Journal* editorial writer, said, "unlike term limits, it doesn't limit democracy, but expands it" by increasing voters' options. The none-of-the-above option allows voters to express their opinions even when they do not support any candidate or when a candidate runs unopposed. Fund supported his argument by citing the 1990 House races in which one in five incumbents had no major party opposition.

Electronic town halls

Another idea, electronic town halls, has received widespread attention thanks to 1992 presidential candidate Ross Perot. The idea, essentially, allows voters to communicate directly with the president or legislators through modern technology, such as by satellite video conferences. In traditional town hall meetings, still used in some places (particularly in New England), townspeople gather in a large meeting place where they debate and then decide on issues of local importance. Town meetings provide true, di-

Bill Clinton at a town meeting in Southfield, Michigan. Televised town meetings have been suggested as a way to get one-on-one contact with the voting public.

rect democracy in which the people—not elected representatives—make the law. Although no one is pushing for national direct democracy, Professor Amitai Etzioni of George Washington University has detailed the advantages of electronic town meetings. Satellite transmissions and television would allow political leaders to reach a large share of the population and to have what he calls meaningful dialogue about issues at electronic town meetings. In other words, representatives could address constituents directly, and constituents could answer directly. They could ask each other questions or seek deeper explanations. According to Etzioni such conversations, with their give-and-take, would give representatives a much better feel for people's concerns than they can get from surveys and polls. He argues that scientific polls require instant and exact answers to difficult issues. Polls also eliminate debate, and the way questions are worded can affect the results. In addition, public meetings tend to develop consensus, or common ground. Etzioni writes:

> The idea deserves serious examination, because if the 1992 election campaign has taught us anything, it's that most Americans feel alienated from national politics as currently practiced, and there is a need to find ways to reinvolve them. . . . Simply changing the cast of characters may not do the trick.

In Great Britain, the public has been discussing other ideas for direct democracy. These ideas include "voter vetoes," which would allow citizens to call a referendum against a law passed by their elected representatives and "voter juries," which would function as citizen advisory groups to the government. In a voter-jury system, a randomly chosen jury would hear evidence on major public issues and then make a recommendation on how the government should handle the issue. "Voter feedback," perhaps by Touch-Tone phone, would enable citizens to express their views on various issues. Variations of these methods exist in democracies around the world. California, for instance, has rules that make it relatively easy for voters to place initiatives on the ballot. The result has been some California elections in which citizens are asked to vote yes or no on numerous ballot questions. In 1990 California voters faced twenty-eight such initiatives.

History has shown that ideas for changing elections often are discussed for years before they gain enough public support to become law. As always, though, changes in U.S. elections are occurring. Time will tell how widespread today's changes will become.

Glossary

absentee ballot: A way of voting intended primarily for people who cannot go to the polls on election day.

delegate: A representative to a convention, including political party conventions.

electorate: A collection of eligible voters.

franchise: The right to vote.

general election: A regularly conducted election, as for filling federal, state, and local offices.

initiative: A referendum on a proposal suggested by a member of the public.

jurisdiction: For elections, the legally defined geographic area in which a candidate is elected.

literacy tests: Tests of reading ability; sometimes used to keep members of minority groups from voting.

nonpartisan election: An election in which candidates are not recognized by party affiliation.

off-year election: A general election in a year in which the presidency is not being decided; also called a midterm election.

platform: Official public policy or philosophy of a political party.

plurality: The largest number of votes, but less than a majority, cast in an election having more than two choices.

political action committee (PAC): A group that allows members to pool their financial resources for political purposes.

political parties: Groups of individuals who join together to seek or keep political power.

poll tax: A tax on people, especially as a requirement for voting; sometimes used to keep members of minority groups from voting.

popular vote: A vote of the people.

primary election: An election to choose candidates for general elections.

proportional representation: An election system in which offices are filled in proportion to votes cast for a selection of parties or candidates.

ratify: To give formal approval; especially, to approve constitutional amendments (and treaties).

referendum: A vote by the people on whether a proposal should become law.

suffrage: The right to vote.

third party: A political party that is not one of the two major parties in a two-party political system.

voter registration: A process that requires people to sign up to vote in advance of an election; intended to avoid fraud.

voter turnout: The proportion of people of voting age who actually vote in a given election.

winner-take-all: An election system in which the candidate with the most votes wins exclusive rights to represent a jurisdiction.

Organizations
to Contact

The following organizations and government offices provide information about elections, campaign practices and financing, candidates, and political parties.

Center for Voting and Democracy
6905 Fifth St. NW, Suite 200
Washington, DC 20012
(202) 882-7378

The center conducts research on and distributes information about alternative electoral systems, particularly proportional representation.

Common Cause
2030 M St. NW, Suite 300
Washington, DC 20036
(202) 833-1200

Common Cause is a political watchdog group that studies and reports on national politics, including campaign finance.

Federal Election Commission
999 E St. NW
Washington, DC 20463
(202) 219-4140
(800) 424-9530

The commission is charged with overseeing the Federal Election Campaign Act and enforcing its rules. It collects campaign finance reports from candidates and political action committees, distributes the public money used for financing presidential election campaigns, and issues reports about campaign finance activity.

League of Women Voters of the United States
1730 M St. NW
Washington, DC 20036
(202) 429-1965

The league is a non-profit group whose main purpose is educating the public about elections. The league has local chapters across the nation that are listed in the telephone books.

Project Vote Smart
129 NW Fourth St. Suite 204
Corvalis, OR 97330
(503) 754-2746

Anyone can contact Project Vote Smart, a nonpartisan, non-profit effort, to get useful and factual information about candidates and elected officials, such as voting records and issue positions.

Public Citizen
2000 P St. NW
Washington, DC 20036
(202) 883-3000

Public Citizen is a governmental watchdog group that maintains lists of congressional votes, including individual members' votes on such issues as campaign finance reform.

U.S. Commission on Civil Rights
624 Ninth St. NW
Washington, DC 20425
(202) 376-8312
(202) 376-8110 (library)

The commission can provide information about discrimination in voting.

County Election Officers
In most states elections are administered by an official at the county level who may be the county clerk or a separately appointed election supervisor or commission.

State Election Officers
The secretary of state in a particular state usually oversees all elections conducted in the state. If the state has an election finance law, the secretary's office also may be responsible for its administration.

Suggestions for Further Reading

Michael Barone and Grant Ujifusa, *The Almanac of American Politics 1994*. Washington, DC: National Journal.

Gene Brown, *The 1992 Election*. Brookfield, CT: Millbrook Press, 1992.

Fred J. Cook, *The Rise of American Political Parties*. New York: Franklin Watts, 1971.

Lee Learner Gray, *How We Choose a President*. 5th ed. New York: St. Martin's Press, 1980.

League of Women Voters of California Education Fund, *Choosing the President 1992*. New York: Lyons & Burford, 1992.

John L. Moore, ed., *Congressional Quarterly's Guide to U.S. Elections*. 3rd ed. Washington, DC: Congressional Quarterly Inc., 1994.

Norman Ornstein and Shirley Elder, *Interest Groups, Lobbying and Policymaking*. Congressional Quarterly Press, 1978.

Thomas R. Raber, *Election Night*. Minneapolis: Lerner Publications, 1988.

Harold W. Stanley and Richard G. Niemi, *Vital Statistics on American Politics*. Washington, DC: Congressional Quarterly Press, 1988.

Margaret C. Thompson, ed., *Presidential Elections Since 1789*. 5th ed. Washington, DC: Congressional Quarterly Inc., 1991.

Additional Works
Consulted

Chuck Alston, "Democrats Flex New Muscle with Trio of Election Bills," *Congressional Quarterly Weekly Report*, March 20, 1993.

Associated Press, "Small Turnout Caused Change," November 10, 1994.

Jennifer Babson and Kelly St. John, "Momentum Helps GOP Collect Record Amounts from PACs," *Congressional Quarterly Weekly Report*, Dec. 3, 1994.

John A. Barnes, "Proportional Deception," *National Review*, July 20, 1992.

James MacGregor Burns, *The Workshop of Democracy*. New York: Knopf, 1985.

William Nisbet Chambers and Walter Dean Burnham, eds., *The American Party Systems*. New York: Oxford University Press, 1975.

Dan Clawson, Alan Neustadtl, and Denise Scott, *Money Talks: Corporate PACs and Political Influence*. New York: BasicBooks, 1992.

Beth Donovan, "Campaign Finance: Election Commission Hearing Revisits Personal Spending," *Congressional Quarterly Weekly Report*, January 15, 1994.

The Economist, "Electoral Reform: Good Government? Fairness? or Vice Versa? Or Both?" May 1, 1993.

The Economist, "Getting Them Out," June 24, 1989.

Amitai Etzioni, "Teledemocracy: The Electronic Town Meeting," *Current*, February 1993.

David Foster, "States Get Creative on Voting," Associated Press, October 24, 1994.

Reuven Frank, "On Television: Election Night," *The New Leader*, October 5–19, 1992.

Sara Fritz and Dwight Morris, *Handbook of Campaign Spending: Money in the 1990 Congressional Races*. Washington, DC: Congressional Quarterly Inc., 1992.

John H. Fund, " 'NOTA' bene," *The New Republic*, November 25, 1991.

Marshall Ganz, "Voters in the Crosshairs: Elections & Voter Turnout," *Current*, May 1994.

Jack W. Germond and Jules Witcover, *Mad as Hell: Revolt at the Ballot Box, 1992*. New York: Warner Books, 1993.

Rederick P. Hart, *Seducing America: How Television Charms the Modern Voter*. New York: Oxford University Press, 1994.

Richard Hofstadter, *The American Political Tradition and the Men Who Made It*. New York: Knopf, 1948.

Dave Kaplan, "Alternative Election Methods: A Fix for a Besieged System?" *Congressional Quarterly Weekly Report*, April 2, 1994.

Montague Kern, *30-Second Politics: Political Advertising in the Eighties*. New York: Praeger, 1989.

John King, "New Party a Real Possibility in '96 Election," Associated Press, October 2, 1994.

Michael Kinsley, "Election Day Fraud on Television," *Time*, November 23, 1992.

Everett Carll Ladd Jr. and Charles D. Hadley, *Transformations of the American Party System*. 2nd edition. New York: W. W. Norton, 1978.

Burdett Loomis, interview with author, 1994.

Frank I. Luntz, *Candidates, Consultants and Campaigns: The Style and Substance of American Electioneering.* Oxford: Basil Blackwell, 1988.

Sarah Orrick, ed., *Congressional Digest.* Washington, DC: Congressional Digest Corp., March 1993.

————, *Congressional Digest.* Washington, DC: Congressional Digest Corp., April 1994.

Ivars Peterson, "Making Votes Count: How to Steal an Election—the Modern Way," *Science News*, October 30, 1993.

Richard H. Pildes, "Gimme Five," *The New Republic*, March 1, 1993.

Gerald M. Pomper and Loretta A. Sernekos, "Why Don't People Vote?" *Current*, October 1991.

Jamin B. Raskin, "Campaign Finance on Trial: Challenging the 'Wealth Primary,'" *The Nation*, November 21, 1994.

Robert Richie, "The Center for Voting and Democracy and Proportional Representation," The Center for Voting and Democracy, Washington, DC, Spring 1995.

Clinton Rossiter, *Seedtime of the Republic.* New York: Harcourt, Brace & World, 1953.

Larry J. Sabato, *The Rise of Political Consultants: New Ways of Winning Elections.* New York: Basic Books, 1981.

Richard Sammon, "Senate Kills Filibuster Threat, Clears 'Motor Voter' Bill," *Congressional Quarterly Weekly Report*, May 15, 1993.

Lisa Scheer, "Mailing It In," *Forbes*, January 25, 1988.

Arthur M. Schlesinger Jr., "Presidential Elections and the Party System," in Arthur M. Schlesinger Jr., ed., *History of American Presidential Elections.* New York: Chelsea House, 1971.

Christopher Schwarz, "Reach Out Elect Someone," *State Government News*, October 1994.

Katharine Q. Seelye, "Debate over Gingrich Tumultuous," *The New York Times*, January 19, 1995.

Richard G. Smolka and Ronald D. Michaelson, "Election Legislation, 1992–93," *The Book of the States*, 1994–95 edition, vol. 30. Lexington, KY: Council of State Governments, 1994.

Frank J. Sorauf, *Inside Campaign Finance: Myths and Realities*. New Haven, CT: Yale University Press, 1992.

Harold W. Stanley and Richard G. Niemi, *Vital Statistics on American Politics*. Washington, DC: Congressional Quarterly Press, 1998.

Bill Turque, "Wiring Up the Age of Technopolitics," *Newsweek*, June 15, 1992.

U.S. News & World Report, "Sea Change," November 21, 1994.

David Van Biema, "One Person, Seven Votes," *Time*, April 25, 1994.

Kae Warnock, "Early Voting," *NCSL Legisbrief*. Denver, CO: National Conference of State Legislatures, November 1994.

Martin P. Wattenberg, *The Decline of American Political Parties, 1952–1980*. Cambridge, MA: Harvard University Press, 1984.

Craig Winneker and Amy Keller, "The Roll Call 50," *Roll Call*, January 23, 1995.

Raymond E. Wolfinger and Steven J. Rosenstone, "Direct Democracy: Back to the Polls," *The Economist*, September 17, 1994.

_____ , *Who Votes*. New Haven, CT: Yale University Press, 1980.

Index

About the Author

Janet Majure is a writer and editor. She has worked as an editor, copy editor, or writer for the *Kansas City Star*, the *Kansas City Times*, the *Denver Post,* and the *Arizona Republic*. She has written for Fodor's Travel Publications. Ms. Majure's freelance articles have appeared in the *Kansas City Star*, the *Denver Post*, the *Chicago Sun-Times*, the *Houston Chronicle*, the *Des Moines Register*, *Kansas!* magazine, *Preservation News*, *Arthritis Today,* and other periodicals. She has also been a copy editor of computer software books published by Macmillan. Ms. Majure lives in Lawrence, Kansas, with her husband, John Lee, and their daughter, Susan Lee.

Picture Credits